AF145507

SHOSTAKOVICH'S
Lady Macbeth of the Mtsensk District

SHOSTAKOVICH'S
Lady Macbeth of the Mtsensk District

PAULINE FAIRCLOUGH

OXFORD
UNIVERSITY PRESS

Oxford University Press is a department of the University of Oxford.
It furthers the University's objective of excellence in research, scholarship,
and education by publishing worldwide. Oxford is a registered trade mark of
Oxford University Press in the UK and in certain other countries.

Published in the United States of America by Oxford University Press
198 Madison Avenue, New York, NY 10016, United States of America.

© Oxford University Press 2025

All rights reserved. No part of this publication may be reproduced, stored in a retrieval system,
transmitted, used for text and data mining, or used for training artificial intelligence, in any form or
by any means, without the prior permission in writing of Oxford University Press, or as expressly
permitted by law, by license or under terms agreed with the appropriate reprographics rights
organization. Inquiries concerning reproduction outside the scope of the above should be sent
to the Rights Department, Oxford University Press, at the address above.

You must not circulate this work in any other form
and you must impose this same condition on any acquirer.

CIP data is on file at the Library of Congress

ISBN 9780197534946 (pbk.)
ISBN 9780197534939 (hbk.)

DOI: 10.1093/9780197534977.001.0001

The manufacturer's authorized representative in the EU for product safety is
Oxford University Press España S.A., Parque Empresarial San Fernando de Henares,
Avenida de Castilla, 2 – 28830 Madrid (www.oup.es/en or product.safety@oup.com).
OUP España S.A. also acts as importer into Spain of products made by the manufacturer.

Series Editor's
INTRODUCTION

Oxford Keynotes reimagines the canons of Western music for the twenty-first century. With each of its volumes dedicated to a single composition or album, the series provides an informed, critical, and provocative companion to music as artwork and experience. Books in the series explore how works of music have engaged listeners, performers, artists, and others through history and in the present. They illuminate the roles of musicians and musics in shaping Western cultures and societies, and they seek to spark discussion of ongoing transitions in contemporary musical landscapes. Each approaches its key work in a unique way, tailored to the distinct opportunities that the work presents. Targeted at performers, curious listeners, and advanced undergraduates, volumes in the series are written by expert and engaging voices in their fields, and will therefore be of significant interest to scholars and critics as well.

In selecting titles for the series, Oxford Keynotes balances two ways of defining the canons of Western music: as lists of works that critics and scholars deem to have articulated key moments in the history of the art, and as lists of works that comprise the bulk of what consumers listen to, purchase, and perform today. Often, the two lists intersect, but the overlap is imperfect. While not neglecting the first, Oxford Keynotes gives considerable weight to the second. It confronts the musicological canon with the living repertoire of performance and recording in classical, popular, jazz, and other idioms. And it seeks to expand that living repertoire through the latest musicological research.

Kevin Bartig
Michigan State University

CONTENTS

ABOUT THE COMPANION WEBSITE

www.oup.com/us/shostakovichladymacbeth

Oxford has created a website to accompany *Shostakovich's Lady Macbeth of the Mtsensk District*, in order to provide material that cannot be made available in a book, namely video examples. The reader is encouraged to consult this resource in conjunction with the text. Examples available online are indicated in the text with Oxford's symbol ⊙.

The reader is invited to explore the full catalog of Oxford Keynotes volumes on the series homepage.
www.oup.com/us/oxfordkeynotes

ACKNOWLEDGMENTS

R ESEARCH FOR THIS BOOK has been kindly funded by a Leverhulme Trust Major Research Fellowship.

Owing to the COVID-19 pandemic that struck in 2020 and then to Russia's brutal invasion of Ukraine in February 2022, I was unable to carry out the research I had planned in Russia. I was, however, immensely fortunate in being sent valuable source materials electronically before and during the pandemic, and I am enormously grateful to friends in Russia and elsewhere who have generously assisted me, especially Olesya Bobrik, who kindly showed me all the extant materials from the Bolshoi's 1935 production during a short visit in 2019, and most of all my dear friend and colleague Olga Digonskaya of the Shostakovich Archive: without her unflagging generosity and support, this book project could not have come to fruition at all. I warmly thank Elizabeth Wilson, who has been a constant source of encouragement and advice and provided many key contacts in the early stages. I would also like to thank Hans-Ulrich Duffek and Gabriel Teschner of Sikorski (now Boosey and Hawkes); Sacha Wagner from Deutsche

Oper am Rhein; Samuel W. Stewart of Special Collections, Addlestone Library, College of Charleston; Sarah Harrison from the Royal Opera House; Mared Browning and Julia Payne of Boosey and Hawkes (London); Andria Hoy of the Cleveland Orchestra Archives; Henrik Lillin and Sonja Heyl of the Dutch National Opera; Yekaterina Ryabkina of the Mikhailovsky Theater; and Larisa Chirkova of the Rostropovich museum-flat, St. Petersburg. I also thank Laurel Fay for very kindly sharing with me part of an especially valuable resource that, in the end, I obtained directly during the 2020 pandemic "window," when archivists strove to make available to researchers materials that they could not access: the director's blocking "score" of Nikolai Smolich's Maly production, written by N. Shulgin and preserved in the St. Petersburg State Museum of Theatre and Music, but with a copy kept in the Mikhailovsky Theater. Although a comprehensive source study of *Lady Macbeth* remains out of reach and would in any case go far beyond the remit of a Keynotes volume, access to these resources has been of critical importance.

For illuminating conversations around performing *Lady Macbeth* and its various roles, I would like to thank Martyn Brabbins, David Pountney, Richard Jones, Josephine Barstow, Christian Badea, Keri-Lynn Wilson, Carole Wilson, Angelina Nikonova, Calixto Bieito, and Eva-Maria Westbroek. My conversations with them have been a joy and a privilege. For supporting my initial idea for this book, I thank the founding editor of the Keynotes series, Kevin Karnes, and for his patience, kindness, and sage editorial input, I am deeply grateful to the present editor, Kevin Bartig, and to both my reviewers, unofficial and official—Caryl Emerson and Marina Frolova-Walker—for their generous engagement and critique, which helped improve the final book immeasurably. The late, and much-missed, Richard Taruskin, a loyal friend to so many of us in Russian music studies, also supported this project generously with a warm reference to the Leverhulme Trust. I would like to thank him here too, even though he is sadly no longer with us.

NOTE ON SOURCES

THROUGHOUT THIS BOOK I refer to key published sources of *Lady Macbeth*, as follows:

Dmitry Shostakovich, *Ledi Makbet Mtsenskogo uezda*, opera v 4-kh deistviakh, 9-ti kartinakh, op. 29. Libretto po N. Leskovu, A. Preys i D. Shostakovich. Moscow: Gosudarstvenniy muzykal'niy teatr imeni narodnogo artista respubliki V. I. Nemirovich-Danchenko, 1933 (piano vocal score, glass print).
Dmitry Shostakovich, *Ledi Makbet Mzenskogo Uezda*, Libretto po Leskovu, A. Preys i D. Shostakovich. Moscow: Muzgiz, 1935 (piano vocal score).
Dmitry Shostakovich, *Lady Macbeth von Mzensk*, Oper in 4 Akten (9 Bildern), Urfassung 1932 (Erstausgabe), Libretto von A. Preis und D. Schostakowitsch nach der gleichnamigen Erzählung von N. Ljeskow, Deutsch von Jörg Morgener und Siegfried Schoenbohm. Klavierauszug. Hamburg: Sikorski, 1979.
Dmitry Shostakovich, *Katerina Ismaylova*, Sobranie sochinenii, vol. 20, 1985 (full orchestral score).

Dmitry Shostakovich, *Ledi Makbet Mtsenskogo Uezda*, Noviy sobranie sochinenii, vol. 53. Moscow: DSCH Publishers, 2011 (piano vocal score).

Dmitry Shostakovich, *Katerina Izmaylova*, Noviy sobranie sochinenii, vols. 58a and 58b. Moscow: DSCH Publishers, 2015 (full orchestral score).

Dmitry Shostakovich, *Ledi Makbet Mtsenskogo Uezda*, Noviy sobranie sochinenii, vols. 52a and 52b. Moscow: DSCH Publishers, 2016 (full orchestral score).

In all references to musical notation, the Helmholz system is used, so that c' = middle C.

It is expected that the reader who wishes to follow musical and textual arguments closely will have access to a printed score. Either the Sikorski score or the New Collected Works score (vols. 52a and 52b) is recommended for this purpose.

The New Collected Works orchestral score of *Lady Macbeth* (vols. 52a and 52b, 2016, editor Irina Levasheva) is the most authoritative complete text of the score. During its compilation, Levasheva consulted all extant manuscript sources in Russia (bar those in the Mariinsky library) and all published scores (including the Sikorski score). Her meticulous commentary and essay included in vol. 52b should be regarded as the most up-to-date source for detailed scholarship on the opera text.

Images used in this book come from the Cleveland opera production of 1935. Though the production used sets designed by Richard Rychtarik and was directed by Wilhelm von Wymetal, the team worked closely with Nikolai Smolich's production notes, compiled for the

Leningrad premiere, and the sets were also based on this and the Nemirovich-Danchenko production. Therefore, images from Cleveland closely mirror those from the original Leningrad and Moscow productions of 1934. The Cleveland Orchestra's conductor Artur Rodziński saw both productions, consulted Shostakovich directly, and brought copies of the materials, including Smolich's production notes and press photographs, back with him to Cleveland.

INTRODUCTION

I FIRST HEARD SHOSTAKOVICH'S *LADY Macbeth of Mtsensk*
as a graduate student in the early 1990s, via Mstislav
Rostropovich's magnificent EMI recording of 1979. I was
blown away by the music's raw power and energy, and its
impact has not lessened for me over the years. However, the
opera is not without its ethical problems: Richard Taruskin
eloquently sketched these in his essay of nearly thirty years
ago, "The Lessons of *Lady M*," with a fierce critique of
Shostakovich's proto-Stalinist celebration of the liquida-
tion of socially undesirable elements by the opera's heroine-
murderess.[1] And there are still other respects in which *Lady
Macbeth* should trouble us today, as well as many things we
do not know about it: how it was understood in its own
time, why its sexual politics are so problematic, and, not
least, the origin of the "original" version of the opera heard
in Rostropovich's recording. Addressing these has been the
motivation for writing this book.

Shostakovich began composing *Lady Macbeth* in 1930,
during an exceptionally challenging period of Soviet cultural history. From around 1928 until the dissolution of

Shostakovich's Lady Macbeth of the Mtsensk District. Pauline Fairclough, Oxford University Press.
© Oxford University Press 2025. DOI: 10.1093/9780197534977.001.0001

all cultural factions in early 1932, militant proletarian arts organizations sought to win total power over artistic life in ugly battles played out in the press and in both public and private denunciations of colleagues.[2] Shostakovich could not afford to alienate them, all the more so since his last opera, *The Nose*, had received harsh criticism from some writers in these organizations.[3] Perhaps because of this added pressure, *Lady Macbeth*, based (like *The Nose*) on a nineteenth-century Russian classic text, was overtly political in a way that *The Nose* was not. Shostakovich took as his basis Nikolai Leskov's rather lurid plot about a young woman (Katerina), unhappily married into a merchant family, who takes a lover (Sergei) and proceeds to murder her father-in-law, husband, and nephew to install her lover as her husband and owner of the business. Finally arrested for her crimes and sent into penal servitude, Katerina murders her rival for Sergei's affection and commits suicide in despair.

This plot was perhaps not, on the face of it, the most inspiring for a young Soviet composer attempting to please a wide cross-section of a Soviet cultural establishment then riven with discord and rivalry. Yet Shostakovich made dramatic changes to Leskov's plot that transformed it into a fable with a distinctly Soviet flavor. Katerina may have been a monster to Leskov, but Shostakovich sought to render her sympathetic to a Soviet audience. The operatic Katerina was restyled into a tragic victim of a loveless marriage and trapped in a stifling environment: estate life in Tsarist Russia. Every character, from the merchant Boris and his son Zinovii down to the humblest worker, is shown to be living in a state of degradation. Katerina, struggling to liberate herself from that world, becomes, if not a proto-Soviet feminist, then at least someone aware of her own humiliated, wasted life. As we will see, Shostakovich bent over backwards to enable his audience to pity her, removing the murder of her nephew completely and making all the other characters around her as hateful as possible. That he did this with music of such irresistible power is the reason the four-act opera was a sensation at its premiere in January 1934 and continued to play to packed houses in Leningrad and Moscow until it was dramatically taken down at Stalin's behest two years later.

The circumstances of the opera's censoring, and their impact on Shostakovich, will be discussed in detail later in this book, but it should be said now that it was an immense shock to him personally. It happened right on the brink of the Stalinist purges that snowballed into what the historian Robert Conquest later called the "Great Terror," in which millions of innocent Soviet citizens lost their liberty and, in many cases, lives.[4] Though Shostakovich understood that there would be no return to grace for this particular opera during Stalin's lifetime, after Stalin died in 1953, he began to plan for its rehabilitation. As we will see, this involved revision and considerable political maneuvering before *Lady Macbeth* was permitted its return to the Soviet stage. The opera had a second life in this revised form and was known internationally not as *Lady Macbeth* but as *Katerina Izmailova*. In this version, as we will see, it enjoyed modest success. It was only after Shostakovich's death in 1975 that Mstislav Rostropovich, exiled from the Soviet Union since 1974, embarked on his dramatic "rediscovery" of what he and the music publisher Hans Sikorski announced to be the "original" opera. In this version, *Lady Macbeth* became the huge operatic hit that it is today.

Lady Macbeth, since Rostropovich relaunched it on the international opera stage with his landmark EMI recording, has been shielded from serious questions about its sexual ethics.[5] Ironically, the source of its present-day protection is the trauma of its censoring following Stalin's visit to a new production in Moscow in January 1936. The opera was harshly criticized in an editorial in the Communist Party paper *Pravda* entitled "Muddle instead of music" (*Sumbur vmesto muzyki*) and removed from the stage.[6] Because this attack came so unexpectedly and ended up being linked with the ensuing purges, music historians have been understandably distracted by the narrative of martyrdom that came to envelop the opera. Yet this backstory was not the only reason for the international acclaim of Rostropovich's rehabilitation of the opera in 1979. In the same year, the young émigré Soviet musicologist Solomon Volkov published what he claimed to be Shostakovich's dictated memoirs, entitled simply *Testimony*.[7] In this explosive (though controversial) book, Volkov's Shostakovich recalled the banishment of *Lady Macbeth* in detail: "Now everyone knew for sure that I would be destroyed. And the anticipation of that noteworthy event . . . has never left me. From that moment I was stuck with the label 'enemy of the people' and I don't need to explain what that label meant in those days. Everyone still remembers that."[8] These two events—the EMI recording of the "original" *Lady Macbeth* and Volkov's revelations—transformed Shostakovich into one of the most talked-about and performed composers of the last century.

And yet, all the documentary evidence we have tells us that Shostakovich's revision of his opera was sincere, and he did not wish *Lady Macbeth* to be revived in its original form. How, then, did it come to pass that in 1979 Rostropovich introduced the world to *Lady Macbeth* in a version that Shostakovich believed he had permanently killed off? An important figure in the opera's complex history was Rostropovich's wife, the soprano Galina Vishnevskaya. She had learned *Katerina Izmailova* when she was preparing for her role in a 1966 film version of the opera (dir. Mikhail Shapiro, Lenfilm), for which she worked with Shostakovich, including singing privately for him parts of the original role from the 1930s score. As I describe in this book, their experience of working together was a revelation for all parties. Vishnevskaya and Rostropovich thus discovered this earlier version of Katerina's part that, according to the composer, no soprano in the 1930s had been able to sing (he had to lower the tessitura in a number of places). They also saw the joy it brought him to hear what he had originally conceived performed with such understanding and artistry. Rostropovich already knew *Katerina Izmailova* well, because he played cello in the orchestra in a 1963 production in Moscow. And in an interview with Solomon Volkov in 1990, Rostropovich made his feelings about the revised opera very clear:

> Both the new version and the revival were by no means masterpieces. I was convinced that a third version ought to come out of it. . . . Together we [Rostropovich and Dmitri Pokrovsky] went to see Comrade Polikarpov, at the Central Committee of the Party, and asked: give us the opportunity to make some

sort of third version based on the first one and that which had been revised (not so much revised as simplified). Give us the opportunity to stage it at the Bolshoi Theatre! . . . Shostakovich, by the way, had accepted, with great pleasure, that we write the final version together. . . . But that never happened.[9]

We will explore how Rostropovich finally achieved his goal of restoring *Lady Macbeth* in chapter 2, but I hope this overview explains why the Cold War context of *Lady Macbeth*'s revival is key to the opera's presence on our opera stages today, and is also the reason very few people ever hear *Katerina Izmailova*, let alone consider that this version might have been the one Shostakovich wanted us to hear. The narrative of the "authentic version" and Stalinist persecution that accompanied Rostropovich's EMI recording, and the score published soon after by Sikorski that almost everyone since 1979 has used, has been too compelling to ignore. The coincidental timing of both the recording and Solomon Volkov's *Testimony* meant that the revival of *Lady Macbeth* went hand in hand with a major international re-evaluation of Shostakovich and his legacy. First came the stage premiere in Wuppertal, Germany, in 1980— apparently initiated before the EMI recording was released but achieved in the end with the score and parts hired out by Sikorski. The first stage performance that was directly inspired by Rostropovich's recording came in the Spoleto Festival in 1980. The young Romanian conductor Christian Badea, then artistic director of the Spoleto Festival (in Italy and in Charleston, South Carolina) who got to know Rostropovich when working as his assistant at the National Symphony Orchestra in Washington, DC, was bowled over

by the EMI recording of *Lady Macbeth*. His conversations
with Rostropovich left him in no doubt whatsoever that the
"original" version of *Lady Macbeth* was the one that repre-
sented Shostakovich's true creative inspiration. Badea recommended *Lady Macbeth* to the president of the Spoleto
Festival, Gian Carlo Menotti, who agreed to its performance. He also commissioned the brilliant Romanian
producer Liviu Ciulei, at that time artistic director of the
Guthrie Theater in Minneapolis, to design the set. After a
nail-biting wait for the score, the Spoleto performance was
a resounding success.[10] So began the opera's triumphal
international march and recognition as a masterpiece the
world over. In a world still divided by the Cold War, *Lady
Macbeth*'s power was political as well as musical; and over
thirty years later, it still is.

The purpose of this short *Keynotes* study, then, is to
peel back some of the layers that have accrued over *Lady
Macbeth*'s reception and production history. Currently, our
knowledge of its Soviet reception in the 1930s is very limited.
So too is our understanding of cultural and social attitudes
to women and sexual violence in Soviet Russia at the time
both when Shostakovich first started planning the opera
and in 1936, the fateful year of Stalin's visit to the Bolshoi
filial production that precipitated the opera's demise. My
aim in writing this volume has been to fill in these gaps
in our knowledge. Above all, it is time to move away
from the unspoken but tangible position that this "original" *Lady Macbeth* is a work beyond criticism. Although
Shostakovich had been a composer enveloped in Cold War
mythology ever since the publication of *Testimony* cast
him variously as a victim, a hero, a tortured genius, and

an embittered dissident, he was nevertheless a real person who made decisions, not all of which were perfect. *Lady Macbeth* is, in some respects, a flawed masterpiece by a young composer who was still learning the art of crafting a libretto from a literary source. Mistakes were made in *Lady Macbeth* that, had the opera not received such a bitter blow, he might have learned from. He was not given that chance. All the same, he revised the opera both during and after rehearsals for the Leningrad and Moscow productions that opened in January 1934, prepared the piano score for publication (Muzgiz, 1935), and revised it again, with the help of his closest friend Isaak Glikman, after Stalin's death. Western opera houses routinely ignore the cuts he made in the 1930s as well as the bigger ones he made later, and those are significant decisions for a director and conductor to make: ones that should not be taken in ignorance of the opera's background and history. For all *Lady Macbeth*'s brilliance, it is an opera of its time, containing music and text that—when we look more closely—rightly cause discomfort today. Confronting that discomfort is what this book is all about.

MAIN *DRAMATIS PERSONAE*

Katerina Izmailova: titular heroine, the beautiful but bored wife of the merchant Zinovii Borisovich Izmailov

Zinovii Izmailov: Katerina's weak-willed husband, bullied by his father and sexually rejected by Katerina

Boris Timofeevich: Zinovii's father, an octogenarian in Leskov's novella but a predatory, violent bully in the opera

Sergei: the new worker in the Izmailov household who seduces Katerina and becomes her lover, then husband

Aksinia: the Izmailov housekeeper

Sonetka: the female prisoner in the transit camp scenes of Act Four, seduced by Sergei when he abandons Katerina

TABLE OF KEY MUSICAL SOURCES REFERRED TO IN TEXT

DATE	TITLE	PUBLISHER/ARCHIVAL LOCATION
1931	*Ledi Makbet Mtsenskogo Uezda.* Draft facsimile (incomplete) of ms (autograph) score	Published in Shostakovich, New Collected Works, Vol. 53, Moscow: DSCH Publishers, 2011, 489–599
1932	*Ledi Makbet Mtsenskogo Uezda.* Autograph score	Russian State Archive of Literature and Art (RGALI), f. 2048, op. 2, ed. khr. 32–35
1933	*Ledi Makbet Mtsenskogo Uezda*	Moscow: Gosudarstvennyi muzykal'nyi teatr imeni narodnogo artista respubliki V. I. Nemirovich-Danchenko, 1933 (piano vocal score, glass print)
1934	*Katerina Izmailova*	Libretto for Nemirovich-Danchenko production
1935	*Ledi Makbet Mtsenskogo Uezda*	Moscow: Muzgiz, 1935. Piano vocal score
1935	*Ledi Makbet Mtsenskogo Uezda*	Copyist's orchestral score, Russian Museum of Musical Culture, Moscow, f. 32, ed. khr. 271

(*continued*)

DATE	TITLE	PUBLISHER/ARCHIVAL LOCATION
1935	*Ledi Makbeth Mtsenskogo Uezda*	Copyist's orchestral score. Russian Museum of Musical Culture, Moscow, f. 32, ed. khr. 284
1979	*Lady Macbeth von Mzensk*	Hamburg: Hans Sikorski Verlag. Piano vocal score

CHAPTER 1

AN OPERA OUT
OF TIME?

S INCE ROSTROPOVICH'S REVIVAL OF *Lady Macbeth*, it
has become commonplace to cite the main reason for
its banishment under Stalin as its shocking sexual content.[1]
This has fed into a general myth that the opera was simply
too controversial for Stalin's Russia, and this has, I believe,
influenced the approach taken by directors right up to the
present day: the sexual shock factor is invariably exaggerated as a way of creating distance from the "puritanical"
cultural norms of Stalinism.

Yet Stalinism was not monolithic but rather an often
unpredictable, febrile cultural and social environment,
where even those closest to power were not always able
to perceive coming changes of policy. *Lady Macbeth* was
not remotely controversial at the time of its creation and

Shostakovich's Lady Macbeth of the Mtsensk District. Pauline Fairclough, Oxford University Press.
© Oxford University Press 2025. DOI: 10.1093/9780197534977.003.0001

premiere, in fact, but it became so overnight in 1936, when official reaction to it served as a decisive indicator of a cultural shift pulling away from any form of modernism in the arts. From that point, it was essential for Soviet commentators to craft a different narrative about it, all but abandoning their previous positions and in some cases being forced to admit to their own flawed judgment for praising it. Despite the fact that the sex scene between Katerina and Sergei—since 1979 considered the dramatic centerpiece of the opera and often directed with frank gusto—was not especially remarked upon by Moscow and Leningrad critics during 1934 and 1935, after the opera's fall from grace, Shostakovich's peers did begin to single out its sexual content as a shortcut for signaling the opera's flaws, as this chapter will show.

A LONG-AWAITED SUCCESS

Lady Macbeth was phenomenally successful in both of the Soviet Russian theaters in which it premiered in 1934: Leningrad's Maly and Moscow's Nemirovich-Danchenko. Both productions ran successfully to packed houses over the next two years: the Leningrad production was staged eighty-three times and the Moscow production ninety-four times in total. In its first year alone, the Leningrad performances ran at over 90% capacity—an astonishing achievement for any new opera.[2] On December 26, 1935, a third production—the Maly on tour—opened in Moscow on the Bolshoi filial stage, using a new set by Vladimir Dmitriev (essentially the Maly set but with some modifications), still directed by Nikolai Smolich but conducted by Alexander Melik-Pashayev. This was the performance that Stalin saw on January 26, 1936.

As we have seen, *Pravda*'s assault on *Lady Macbeth* meant that it was quickly removed from the repertoire. But although Shostakovich seems to have concluded that his opera was finished, there were others in the cultural world whose opinion differed. *Lady Macbeth*'s success was so exceptional that some sought to resolve the debacle by writing directly to Stalin or finding other ways to circumvent *Pravda*'s judgment. For instance, Levon Atovmian, a good friend of Shostakovich's, gained the consent of the Bolshoi director, Elena Malinovskaia, to seek permission from members of the Central Committee to perform Act Four of the opera at the Bolshoi in a special performance showcasing Shostakovich's most successful works. Shostakovich, however, was less than enthusiastic. In Atovmian's recollection, Shostakovich had said something like, "And why do you need to arrange this ending? Is the outcome of all this not clear to you? The public, of course, will applaud— after all, it is considered 'good form' to be in opposition among us—and then another article will appear under some heading like 'incorrigible formalist.' Is that what you are trying to achieve?"[3] Maxim Gorky, who famously wrote to Stalin on Shostakovich's behalf, allegedly rubbished *Pravda*'s editorial in his letter with a frankness that suggests that he thought Shostakovich might be quickly forgiven.[4] The composer's other distinguished friend, the Red Army Marshal Mikhail Tukhachevsky, wrote to Stalin as well: an act of kindness carried out under unimaginable stress. Shostakovich recalled that Tukhachevsky's face ran with sweat as he wrote the letter: it seems that he understood better than Gorky who had authorized it.⁵ It took time too for Shostakovich's loyal friends and colleagues in the Leningrad branch of the Composers' Union to succumb to political pressure to condemn *Lady Macbeth*. In the earliest meeting in Leningrad (February 5) called to discuss the *Pravda* article, the musicologists Ivan Sollertinsky (Shostakovich's then-closest friend) and Alexander Rabinovich publicly defended the opera; it was not until a later four-day meeting held between February 21 and 26 that Sollertinsky recanted under pressure. Shostakovich's friend Isaak Glikman remembered that in advance of the meeting, Sollertinsky confided that Shostakovich had authorized him to say whatever he felt was needed to secure his own (Sollertinsky's) personal survival.⁶ His speech was reported in the Composers' Union journal *Sovetskaia muzyka* in May 1936, and despite what we know of their private agreement, it makes for sad reading. In the clichéd language so common for those fraught times (abandoning his usually sophisticated critical voice), Sollertinsky publicly decried the opera he loved:

> I overlooked a number of the basic elements of petit-bourgeois expressionism. First of all, I overlooked the erotic element, which flourished particularly in Berg, being especially clear in the animal passion between Marie and the Sergeant Major (which later led Berg to the erotic-hysterical opera Lulu) and this was completely transferred to the relationship between Sergei and Katerina Izmailova in Shostakovich's opera. . . . From Berg, sexuality passed to Shostakovich, not in the form of frivolous eroticism, but with a serious metaphysical purpose. . . . I failed to notice the petit-bourgeois, anarcho-individualistic element that crept into Shostakovich's music.⁷

As we will see, however, although the ramifications of *Pravda*'s attack did eventually sink in even among the most optimistically inclined supporters of Shostakovich, there was good reason for their initial hesitation: the unanimous critical praise of the opera up until the *Pravda* article. From its first public outings (Leningrad composers had followed its progress eagerly from 1932), *Lady Macbeth* had been hailed as the work that would address the dearth of Soviet operas.

It was especially challenging for artists to create Soviet opera that could rank alongside the classical and romantic repertory that dominated the contemporary stage; Soviet ballet had the same problem. Imperial-era Russian opera standards such as Tchaikovsky's *Evgeny Onegin*, Rimsky-Korsakov's fairytale operas, and Musorgsky's epic *Boris Godunov* remained staples of Soviet operatic culture. Some of the most popular Western classics in the early Soviet era included Smetana's *Bartered Bride*, Bizet's *Carmen*, and several Wagner operas, including *Lohengrin* and *Die Meistersinger*.[8] Competing on any serious level with this heritage was near impossible for all but the most gifted Soviet composers. And the stakes for getting such a high-profile genre wrong were far higher than for orchestral and chamber music; even Shostakovich had seen his first opera *The Nose* close earlier than it would otherwise have done owing to pressure from the militant proletarian wing of Soviet musical circles.[9]

There had been a handful of modestly successful Soviet operas, discounting experiments in supplying Soviet libretti to established classics such as the reworking of Puccini's *Tosca* as *Battle for the Commune*.[10] Soviet audiences had been treated to Arseny Gladkovsky and Evgeny Prussak's co-composed *For Red Petrograd* in 1925, Vassily Zolotarev's *Decembrists* in the same year, Shostakovich's *The Nose* in 1929, and Lev Knipper's *North Wind* at the Bolshoi in 1930.[11] But there had been nothing comparable to *Lady Macbeth*. Although it did not have the built-in ideological merit of being based on a revolutionary theme, *Lady Macbeth* was recognized as deliberately moving away from the avant-gardism of *The Nose* toward a more lyrical, expressive language that could reasonably be expected to have mass appeal. Its ideological orientation was also regarded as appropriately Soviet, although not without reservations, as we will see. But its seriousness of purpose, its expressive accessibility, and its dramatic impact were all acknowledged in the cultural press, by Shostakovich's peers and by audiences too.

SOVIETIZING THE CLASSICS

In adopting a socially and politically critical approach to Nikolai Leskov's 1865 novella, Shostakovich was following in the steps of the revolutionary Russian theater director Vsevolod Meyerhold. Trained in the realist methods of Konstantin Stanislavsky and Vladimir Nemirovich-Danchenko, Meyerhold by 1920 had founded his own theater, which became a crucible for the most innovative approaches to stage acting of the last century. Though he is today mostly remembered for his acting system known as biomechanics, for our purposes his more intriguing innovation lies in the way he approached the classics critically, bringing contemporary Soviet ideology to bear on traditional narratives. To this end, he would stage older (prerevolutionary) plays but take steps to prevent the audience from viewing the spectacle passively with techniques designed to "defamiliarize" or "make strange" well-known works and thus activate the spectator's critical faculties.[12] This could take the form of juggling around acts and scenes so that the narrative chronology was broken, allowing Meyerhold to focus instead on an aspect of characterization or plot; it could also involve cutting or adding to sections of a play to bring a contemporary critical lens to bear directly on its familiar narrative.[13] Shostakovich knew Meyerhold and admired his theater immensely; he had stayed as a guest in Meyerhold's household in Moscow for a time, and even played piano in his staging of Vladimir Mayakovsky's *The Bedbug* (for which Shostakovich also supplied music). In the wake of "Muddle instead of music," Meyerhold took the unimaginably brave step of defending Shostakovich publicly as well as supporting him privately.[14]

In taking his own "defamiliarizing" approach to Leskov, Shostakovich also sought to prime his contemporaries' eyes and ears to what he believed was ideologically flawed in the novella. To Shostakovich's Soviet-trained mind, Katerina Lvovna was neither a serial killer nor a monster, but a tragic victim. He imagined a passionate, sensitive woman trapped in a loveless marriage, her talents and personality squandered in a life of degrading idleness. Encountering life-changing passion for the first time in her short life, Katerina acts upon her desires in a way that is presented in the opera as courageous rather than immoral. She is caught, imprisoned, and sent into penal servitude along with her former lover Sergei, finally consigning herself to death as she commits her final murder.

Working together with his librettist Alexander Preis, Shostakovich subjected Leskov's story to alterations of Meyerholdian proportions: Katerina's unremarkable husband Zinovii is turned into a contemptible figure, bullied by his father and—as suggested by both music and libretto—impotent (Leskov's story also suggests this, as Katerina becomes pregnant by Sergei, and the prior lack of an Izmailov heir is said to have been a cause of sadness in the household).[15] The figure of her father-in-law Boris Timofeevich is grotesquely transformed: the original eighty-year-old Boris is now shown to lust after Katerina and even to consider seducing her himself, neither of which we have any inkling of in Leskov. Sergei, a standard-issue chancer eager to advance himself, becomes a callous, abusive male who thinks nothing of tormenting and even raping a woman. The little nephew that they both murder in Leskov's telling—for the sole purpose of getting their hands on the Izmailov fortune—is removed from the story entirely to prevent the audience from losing patience with Katerina's violent crimes; the murder of a child was a boundary of tolerance audiences would not want to cross.

Shostakovich felt that such a radical rewrite required proper explanation. And he obliged, in several pieces written for the Soviet press and for the Leningrad and Moscow program booklets. As early as 1932, he explained in the cultural periodical *Sovetskoe iskusstvo* that

the subject of Lady Macbeth [is] . . . the truthful and tragic depiction of the fate of a talented, intelligent and outstanding woman perishing in the nightmarish conditions of pre-revolutionary Russia. . . . Apart from the fact that Ekaterina Lvovna murders her husband and father in law, she is nevertheless a sympathetic figure. I tried to cast her whole environment in a negative, satirical light. I do not recognise the word "satirical" as "funny" or "mocking." On the contrary, in Lady Macbeth I tried to create a kind of satire that exposes, tearing off masks and creating hatred for the terrible abuses of merchant life.[16]

When Shostakovich wrote these words, Act Four of his opera remained unfinished. But he made clear—at least so he thought—what kind of satire he was using, and for what purpose. The almost comic-strip approach taken to the scene with the policemen in Act Three (entirely a Preis-Shostakovich creation), for instance, bears the stamp of typical 1920s Soviet satire, with their plaintive refrain "Where could we make the extra bob/If we didn't fiddle on the job."[17] Agitprop posters routinely used humorous-looking cartoons to make deadly serious points: the bourgeois banker growing fat on his exploitation of workers was just one of many standard tropes. The lazy, corrupt police in *Lady Macbeth*, just like the drunken priest (also a Preis-Shostakovich addition), are classic stooges of 1920s Soviet comic theater and poster campaigns. For priests, who found themselves on the frontlines of Lenin's hostile actions against the church, such campaigns could be deadly, and village priests could find themselves publicly defrocked and humiliated, forced to renounce their faith and "admit" to deceiving parishioners.[18] But the starkly drawn heroes and villains of Soviet propaganda campaigns were all grist to Shostakovich's mill as he and Preis reinvented Leskov's tale for the new age. In two lucidly argued essays written for the opera's premieres entitled "My understanding of 'Lady Macbeth'" (*Moe ponimanie 'Ledi Makbet'*) for the Leningrad Maly and "About my opera" (*O moey opere*) for the Nemirovich-Danchenko in Moscow, Shostakovich explained his approach in more detail[19]:

> My "Lady Macbeth of Mtsensk" was conceived in quite a different way to Leskov's. . . . Leskov, as a pre-revolutionary writer, was unable to give the correct interpretation to the events he describes in his story.
>
> My role, as a Soviet composer, was to approach the story critically, and to adopt a Soviet perspective while keeping the strengths of Leskov's tale. Therefore I made some changes. We might recall from Leskov's story that Ekaterina Lvovna Izmailova commits three murders before she is sent into penal servitude (she kills her father-in-law, husband and little nephew). As I wished to acquit Ekaterina Lvovna of guilt so that the spectator would gain a sympathetic understanding of her, I removed the nephew's murder, which she committed for mercenary reasons (in order to inherit the estate after her husband's murder). I tried to make Ekaterina Lvovna a positive character with whom the audience would sympathise. To achieve this sympathy was far from easy: Ekaterina Lvovna carries out several deeds that are incompatible with ethical and moral values. This is the basis of my departure from Leskov: Leskov draws Ekaterina Lvovna as a cruel woman driven mad by boredom who murders people who are, in Leskov's view, innocent. But I prefer to explain the events in this way: Ekaterina Lvovna is an intelligent, talented and interesting woman; because of the stifling and nightmarish conditions of her life, surrounded by the cruel and greedy merchant milieu, her life has become sad, dull and bitter. She does not love her husband and she has no

means of fun or amusement. Then suddenly the clerk Sergei appears, whom her husband Zinovii Borisovich has engaged. It turns out that she falls in love with him; though he is an entirely negative and worthless character, this love brings to her life meaning and joy. To be with Sergei, she then commits several crimes. When Boris Timofeevich, Ekaterina Lvovna's father-in-law, catches Sergei after he has been with Katerina and orders him to be flogged, she burns for revenge and poisons her father-in-law for what he has done to her lover. And later, when Sergei tells her that he doesn't want to be her secret lover but rather her husband, Ekaterina Lvovna tells him it will be so, and when Zinovi Borisovich returns after a long journey, she and Sergei together strangle him to remove the last obstacle to their path to happiness.

[. . .] Ekaterina Lvovna, in her love for Sergei, sacrifices herself entirely. Outside of her love for Sergei nothing exists for her. When, after their crimes, she and Sergei are sent into penal servitude and she believes he has abandoned her for the convict Sonetka, she suffers dreadfully and tragically drowns both herself and Sonetka in the river, since life without Sergei holds no meaning for her.[20]

Such a conception of Katerina was far removed from Leskov's depraved antiheroine, as Caryl Emerson and Richard Taruskin have both argued.[21] And Shostakovich himself makes it clear that his Katerina and Leskov's are essentially different characters: he used Leskov's tale as a basis, a sequence of events and characters, but completely reinterpreted it to deliver an impeccable Soviet fable. As he explained, Leskov, by virtue of his prerevolutionary perspective, had been simply "unable to give the correct interpretation," and Shostakovich's self-appointed job was to correct Leskov's limited worldview by expanding the philosophical horizons of *Lady Macbeth* with a contemporary Soviet perspective. In Shostakovich's new reading, Katerina Lvovna would be entirely justified in struggling to free herself from the degraded life of the prerevolutionary merchant class, whose representatives are given appropriately distasteful coloring. To fully engage the audience's sympathy, she would also have her character's ruthless determination altered substantially. In the Maly program booklet, Shostakovich referred approvingly to a "leading musician" who had called Katerina a Desdemona or Juliet of Mtsensk, since rather than being like Shakespeare's "energetic" Lady Macbeth, Katerina is "gentle [*miagkii*], suffering, arousing not fear but regret, pity and sympathy."[22]

CONTEMPORARY CRITICAL PERSPECTIVES BEFORE 1936

Most Soviet critics fully grasped and accepted Shostakovich's intentions and motivation, a reality obscured in the wake of *Pravda*'s extreme response. Although the author of the *Pravda* article, David Zaslavsky, sneered that "Leskov's story is given a significance it does not possess" and complained about Katerina being presented as "some kind of victim," his ultra-literal response in *Pravda* to *Lady Macbeth* was out of step with other critical voices in Leningrad's and Moscow's cultural scene. Indeed, as we will see, before he received this commission, Zaslavsky, at least in hindsight, claimed that he felt unable to voice criticism of the opera in the face of such overwhelmingly positive consensus. Certainly, any criticism of *Lady Macbeth*'s ideological positioning prior to Zaslavsky's article was at a level of sophistication far in excess of what was subsequently displayed after the *Pravda* editorial had been published.

One of the authors commissioned to write in the program booklet for the Nemirovich-Danchenko production was the musicologist Alexander Ostretsov. He was not a member of Shostakovich's circle and would not explicitly defend Shostakovich after the *Pravda* attack, though he refrained from condemning *Lady Macbeth* during the meetings convened to discuss it.[23] Ostretsov had favorably previewed *Lady Macbeth* in a long analytical piece for *Sovetskaia muzyka* in 1933, and he also contributed two fine essays to the Nemirovich-Danchenko libretto entitled "Russia in the 1840s" (about Leskov's ideological positioning) and "The music of the opera."[24] In his 1933 article for *Sovetskaia muzyka*, Ostretsov went to considerable lengths to explain his most serious ideological criticism of the new opera, and it was on Act Four that he focused his objections:

Shostakovich interprets the criminal world of bandits, murderers, thieves, arsonists and horse thieves in terms of a kind of epic House of the Dead, accepting punishment for their crimes, as though hard labor was an inevitable evil in life. The image of the convicts is one of "unfortunates," unhappy people with constrained will and hopelessness in their heart. Siberia imposes on them passivity and Christian obedience. We are far from blaming Shostakovich and Preis for not depicting criminals as carriers of ideas of the revolutionary underground and for not turning them into political exiles, conscious fighters against tsarism. It goes without saying that socially degraded types, like the prostitute Sonetka or Sergei himself, in no way can be compared with the courageous, staunch fighters against the autocracy. But this in no way justifies an undifferentiated approach to hard labor and convicts, summarizing all hard labor in the image of a resigned convict, clanking their shackles and slavishly accepting a beating from their tormentors. We cannot agree with such an interpretation of penal servitude . . . [for] not finding colors for anger, unquenchable resistance and the fight against the age-old oppression of the bloody regime and the social order that gave rise to it. Such interpretation distorts historical reality. . . . [I]t facilitates passivity and belief in . . . the iron logic of the historical process. . . . [H]ard labor was not only a place of suffering, but was also the [place of] constant fermentation . . . and the inexorable will to protest and struggle.[25]

I quote Ostretsov at length here because it seems to me that his objection is rooted in a very specific kind of Soviet worldview: one that is more profoundly weighted toward Marxist-Leninist philosophy than Shostakovich's. It gets to the very nub of what was *not* in fact especially "Soviet" about this opera, despite Shostakovich consciously striving to rework his nineteenth-century source in true Meyerholdian style.

Shostakovich's casting of this fallen woman as a victim of the social conditions that any upright Soviet citizen would be expected to regard with loathing might superficially strike us as quintessentially "Soviet." But although his contemporaries acknowledged this ideological strategy, they were not necessarily ready to embrace it wholesale. Critics might have stopped short of sympathizing with the murdered merchant family, but they found other ideological weaknesses. Ostretsov is correct to say that by casting Katerina as the only positive character and the penal colony as an (almost) undifferentiated mass of human misery, Shostakovich missed the opportunity to acknowledge that Tsarist-era penal colonies were not composed only of criminals: his perspective of overarching pity was, ideologically speaking, insufficiently alert to the dangers of passive acceptance of suffering. Glimpses into convict life—centered only upon Katerina and Sergei—show only more cruelty, although in Leskov there is actually more differentiation. In the original tale, Katerina is comforted by a sympathetic female convict, Fiona, and defended against Sergei's abuse by another male, the kindly Gordiushka (perhaps the inspiration for the Preis-Shostakovich Old Convict). It is possible that Shostakovich took some of this criticism on board when, in the 1950s, he revised the opera and added a final rhetorical question to the Old Convict's lines at the very end: "Akh, why is our life so dark and terrible?/Was man really born for such a life?" A nod, also, to Sonetka's more nuanced character—conceived by Shostakovich as less cruel than the score and libretto alone could show—comes in Mikhail Shapiro's 1966 film of the opera. In the terrible last moment before Katerina pushes Sonetka overboard to her death, Sonetka turns to her rival with a conciliatory gesture. Without that small, fruitless gesture of rough kindness, Sonetka's portrayal too easily remains that of a heartless convict: something that we know exasperated Shostakovich when he saw singers failing to grasp that she too was to be pitied (figure 1.1).[26]

Ostretsov's objection that Shostakovich's portrayal of the penal colony was more humanist, even quasi-Christian, than Marxist-Leninist was taken up by other Soviet critics once the opera had opened. It was, in fact, the most

FIG. 1.1 Act Four, Scene Nine: Sonetka mocks Katerina. Cleveland production, 1935. Photo by Geoffrey Landesman, courtesy of The Cleveland Orchestra Archives.

sustained of contemporary Soviet criticisms of the opera before 1936. Even Shostakovich's former close friend Valerian Bogdanov-Berezovsky felt the total absence of any socially progressive or redeeming characters in the opera to be a distortion of historical perspective.[27] While it was expected that Leskov would not have provided such glimpses of future hope, it was reasonable to feel that a Soviet artist might have done so, especially in Act Four, where Leskov had actually painted his prisoners in more varied ways than Shostakovich had done. Ostretsov doubled down on his own earlier criticism when he went to review the opera at the Nemirovich-Danchenko Theater. Although his review was broadly positive, he alluded to the "barren, useless humanism" of Shostakovich's depiction of the penal colony."[28]

Although Ostretsov was more friendly than hostile toward Shostakovich's opera, his complaint about *Lady Macbeth*'s "humanism"—initially touted as part of Shostakovich's move toward more lyrical and expressive language—could also function as shorthand for signaling the opera's lack of political credentials. During discussions among Leningrad musical circles before the premiere, lines were drawn between Shostakovich's allies and those who adopted a more critical stance. In February 1934, the Leningrad branch of the Composers' Union held meetings to discuss the new opera, reported in the May issue of *Sovetskaia muzyka*. The issue opened with a substantial review of these discussions and those which had already taken place in 1933, coauthored by the Leningrad branch chair Vladimir Iokhelson and Viktor Gorodinsky.[29] Elements of Ostretsov's critique recur here: Iokhelson and Gorodinsky allude rather scornfully to the notion of a "Beatrice or Desdemona of Mtsensk" (mangling the original tribute), accusing Shostakovich of ignoring the real social conditions of Mtsensk itself and, in focusing all his attention on Katerina, stripping her of her historical context, offering only a "wholly humanistic and idealistic conception of 'humanity.'"[30] The notion of Katerina as "classless" had been advanced by the chair of the Composers' Union and editor of *Sovetskaia muzyka* Nikolai Cheliapov, which perhaps explains the column inches given it in this report. In truth this observation is rather unfair. Katerina's class background (wife of a wealthy merchant) is surely clear, although perhaps what Cheliapov really meant was that she did not behave in a way that either typified or challenged her class identity, but purely as an emotionally driven human being. Essentially, these criticisms all stem from the same dissatisfaction with Shostakovich's portrayal of the working class and convict camp: all are degraded, and all are pitiful. None embody any kind of social awareness or carry a grain of hope for a better future. And Katerina herself, despite Shostakovich's Sovietized rendering of Leskov's story, is in no way a prototype for any kind of New Soviet Woman. Entirely consumed by desire and the need to secure Sergei's devotion, she commits murder upon murder until all is lost to her. The message of *Lady Macbeth* was indeed a very human one; and, Meyerholdian caricatures aside, it was not, in truth, an especially "Soviet" one if, like Ostretsov, critics wished to see a clear Marxist-Leninist social and historical perspective at work.

Was this to be the ideological stumbling block on which Soviet reception of Shostakovich's opera would founder? Most certainly not: *Lady Macbeth* was (by then) far too big to fail, as even the most hostile members of the Composers' Union would have granted. But we see something else going on at this point that reveals the nature of ideological dividing lines between Leningrad's and Moscow's musical camps. Iokhelson and Gorodinsky turn sharply from their minor ideological criticisms of the opera to a full-scale critique, not of Shostakovich or of *Lady Macbeth* at all, but of Shostakovich's friend and champion, the musicologist and well-known critic and lecturer Ivan Sollertinsky.

It is at this point that undercurrents of real antipathy begin to emerge from the historical record. Sollertinsky was deeply resented by some figures in the Leningrad Composers' Union branch for his advocacy of Western modernism, and the specific nature of his support for *Lady*

Macbeth brought matters to a head. He had always been known as someone whose musical tastes many considered radical, even unpatriotic (he even devised a plan to lure the newly exiled Arnold Schoenberg from the United States to the Moscow Conservatoire, which, happily for Schoenberg, never came to fruition), but he caused severe offense when he downplayed *Lady Macbeth*'s debt to Russian musical heritage in his program booklet essay for the Leningrad Maly production.[31] This provoked a snarl from Iokhelson and Gorodinsky—"It is not for nothing that Alban Berg is counted among the spiritual fathers of Shostakovich by Sollertinsky while dismissing his kinship with Russian music as near-total"—although in fact Sollertinsky had never made this claim quite so baldly.[32] Sollertinsky's essay had identified three major strands in Shostakovich's creative evolution. The first of these was Russian academicism, explained by the influence of his teacher Maximilian Steinberg and considered now to be "negligible" in Shostakovich's music, although further examples of "recidivism" could be heard in the Second Symphony and in the ballets. The charge of "recidivism" was probably intended as a joke, but it was a joke with a target all the same: the "academic" inheritors of Nikolai Rimsky-Korsakov and his school. The second strand of influence was, Sollertinsky said, Igor Stravinsky, while the third was German symphonism, via Alban Berg (in the form of using classical musical forms such as fugue, passacaglia, and chaconne) and Gustav Mahler.

Sollertinsky's positioning of Shostakovich as a composer who had moved far from the sphere of influence of his Conservatoire mentors and its distinguished first professor of composition, Nikolai Rimsky-Korsakov, enraged a section of the Leningrad Composers' Union, as can be seen from Iokhelson and Gorodinsky's response:

> For Sollertinsky, the primary source of Shostakovich's creative genesis was the paths offered by the West, and specifically "Western modernism." . . . Just as a magnetic compass always points north, Sollertinsky always returns to the West. . . . Sollertinsky mentions Tchaikovsky, Musorgsky and Borodin, but only to emphasise Shostakovich's distance from them, acknowledging only a kinship with Tchaikovsky—but again only in terms of technical manner—affinity as a "creatively productive type."[33]

Although it is tempting to write off this reaction as nothing more than dull xenophobia and hurt pride, we should not overlook the fact that blithely writing off the Conservatoire's role in forming Leningrad's brightest musical star was guaranteed to cause offense, all the more so as Sollertinsky was obviously overstating his case. A significant number of reviews of *Lady Macbeth*—both Soviet and Western—note Shostakovich's strong debt to Musorgsky in Act Four. For this reason, putting aside the obvious viciousness directed at Sollertinsky in this report, the anger voiced here is not easily dismissed.

Nevertheless, throughout 1934 and 1935 the Leningrad Composers' Union knew they had a composer in whom they could take immense pride. And Iokhelson did not, in fact, intend to offer any serious critique of *Lady Macbeth*. In the July 1934 issue of *Sovetskaia muzyka*, he praised the opera warmly, claiming that it marks Shostakovich's "maturity" after the expressionism of *The Nose*; and in the first issue that year (January 1934) he had already praised Shostakovich fulsomely for "using his great powers to reveal the social types of the period, creating moments that are tragic, which brilliantly expose and ridicule the absurdities of the tsarist social system."[34] It was not Shostakovich but rather Sollertinsky who provoked anger and hostility in the Leningrad Composers' Union branch, and beyond it too. The Moscow branch included some prominent and well-loved composers who fell squarely into Sollertinsky's definition of "academic" composers, chief among them Nikolai Miaskovsky, whom Sollertinsky had already openly insulted by referring to "Miaskovshchina" as shorthand for everything that he considered dull and provincial in Soviet music.[35] Accusing Sollertinsky of "modernist revanchism," Iokhelson reminded composers that they were "waging war against . . . the resurrection of the traditions of modernist formalism." Evidently confident that his audience would be sympathetic, he continued sarcastically, "Comrade Sollertinsky will indignantly ask us where we see recurrences of modernist revanchism?—In your articles, dear comrade Sollertinsky, and above all in the article about 'Lady Macbeth' in the program booklet of the Maly Opera House!"[36]

Despite the lively presence of Western modernism in Leningrad Philharmonia schedules during the mid-1930s, tensions between those who openly championed such music and those who remained hostile had never gone away.[37] The most powerful organization of this hostile wing, the militant Russian Association of Proletarian Musicians (RAPM), had been stripped of its legitimacy by the Resolution "On the Reconstruction of Literary and

Artistic Organisations" of April 23, 1932, which liquidated all cultural factions and replaced them with a clear unionized structure. On the face of it, this appeared to put an end to the turbulence of Soviet musical life caused by an aggressive proletarian wing (which could be both viciously anti-Western and anti–avant-garde) and a mostly centrist majority who found themselves attacked by the RAPM on multiple fronts.[38] It is true, as Sheila Fitzpatrick has shown, that even during the post–"Muddle instead of music" discussions of *Lady Macbeth*, any attempt to revive the fortunes of the proletarian militants in the Composers' Union was immediately shut down, both in the live discussions and subsequently in the press—even in *Pravda* itself.[39] But equally, it was by no means the case that the power wielded by Sollertinsky (then artistic advisor to the Leningrad Philharmonia) made him untouchable. The newly created Composers' Union was a broad church, comprising all former factions, from the most hard-line proletarians to internationalists like Sollertinsky, and debates on such major issues as a new opera by Shostakovich were inevitably going to be robust.

On the one hand, Composers' Union leaders were anxious to give due praise to the opera (and take indirect credit for its success), and the fact that Shostakovich had turned away from the radical modernism familiar to them from his first opera *The Nose* and other works of the late 1920s was universally applauded. *Lady Macbeth*'s more expressive language was praised in many of the press reviews. But the empty charge of "formalism" (shorthand for using language considered to be too difficult for the mass listener, with the implied accusation of undue Western influence) had never lost its sting from the RAPM era. Iokhelson's take-down of Sollertinsky shows that, even in 1934, the militant elements of the Composers' Union were poised to revisit the old battle sites even if they were not prepared to allow some of the more vociferous warriors (such as Lev Lebedinsky) back into positions of power. As we will see, these simmering tensions and resentments exploded into outright warfare in the heated post-"Muddle" discussions, when some of those formerly insulted (even if only indirectly) by Sollertinsky, such as Shostakovich's former Conservatoire teacher Maximilian Steinberg, were only too happy to set on record their antipathy for Shostakovich's music. Ultimately, the insults of the RAPM era ("formalist," "degenerate," "alien to the masses") coalesced into standard critical tropes of the post-1932 Stalin period. In hindsight we can see that the *Lady Macbeth* discussions proved to be a crucible for the re-establishment of these same poisonous epithets as standard terminology.

LADY MACBETH'S *RISE AND FALL*

In 1934, salvos against Sollertinsky bounced off both him and Shostakovich: once *Lady Macbeth* opened in Leningrad and Moscow, its sheer popularity overwhelmed these old grudges and there was little space left for those who wished to carp. The snapshot of Soviet reviews given here is a fair survey of the plaudits showered upon the opera.[40] Following a preview of the first three acts in 1932, the arts magazine *Sovetskoe iskusstvo* ran a trio of articles on the opera (including one by Shostakovich), and here the critic Mattias Grinberg singled out the scenes with workers, police, and the wedding feast because "they are the first not to idealise the lives of the working people, as was so typical in for example Tchaikovsky's *Evgeny Onegin* and the work of the kuchkists [the so-called "Mighty Handful"], but instead show real life and its hopelessness in Nikolaevan Russia, punctuated by savagery."[41] Just as importantly, Grinberg highlighted the expressivity of Shostakovich's musical language. His review is one of the most eloquent in praising the opera's lyrical force:

> The magnificent entr'acte between the fourth and fifth scenes is utterly Bachian. And at the start of this act, the night scene between Ekaterina and Sergei, we have beautiful pages of the "new" Shostakovich. We have listed several of the most remarkable places, but there are so many exciting moments in *Lady Macbeth* we cannot count them all: the whole of Act 2, the scene with Ekaterina Lvovna in Act 1, in Act 3 the song of a sloppy drunk, the wedding, the scene of the bride and groom's capture with a complex fugue, the portrayal of disgusting drunken revelry—these instances contain the most beautiful, memorable music.[42]

In a later issue, Grinberg previews the Nemirovich-Danchenko production specifically, and here he becomes more critical as he discusses Shostakovich's stated intention of recasting Katerina's story through a Soviet lens to awaken contemporary sympathy. Like Ostretsov, Grinberg doubts Shostakovich has succeeded in his aim, but for Grinberg it is the emphasis on sexual activity and motivation that overshadow social comment:

In his numerous preliminary statements about Izmailova, Shostakovich invariably asserted that in Leskov's Lady Macbeth he was inspired by the social tragedy of a Russian woman—a talented, bright, strong woman who perishes in the "stinking dungeon" of Russian life. . . . But the theme of social tragedy for Shostakovich turned out to be complicated by another theme—an erotic theme. . . . For Shostakovich, the love drama acquired a self-sufficient meaning in the opera. Moreover, almost all the characters in the opera are involved in one way or another in the "love" theme. . . . For Katerina and Sergey, this is dramatically true, but the old father-in-law Boris Timofeevich turns out to be an erotomaniac in the opera too. A playboy in his youth . . . in the autumn of his days he only dreams of how to hang around after Katerina. The main theme here is that Katerina has "no man, no man"—he repeats this obsessively. When he equips his son for the road, he only talks to him about Katerina's possible betrayal. . . . The mass scene in the second scene—the workers' horseplay with Aksinia— also revolves "around love." Love interests overshadow all other everyday interests in Shostakovich's opera. The theme of love pushes aside the theme of social tragedy in Katerina Izmailova.[43]

Nevertheless, Grinberg does not complain about the Act One sex scene itself; his observation is merely that the opera's sexual focus overwhelms its function as social commentary. And crucially, Grinberg is in no doubt that Shostakovich has more than overcome his former preoccupation with Western peers:

Images of living people now appear in Shostakovich's work. . . . [T]he convicts on stage are presented with moving sincerity, and are given warmth and humanity. In this sense, Act Four of the opera is exceptional. . . . It bears the influence of the classics and Russian music of the past, overcoming the constructivist contemporary Western European influences. It is extremely important to emphasize that this new musical direction, Shostakovich's new style, is connected precisely with his craving for a major theme, for socially saturated content, for a living person. Here one cannot fail to see yet another proof of the complete collapse of modern musical ideas and modern practice —their alienation and hostility to Soviet musical creativity. Such are the main tendencies and features of Shostakovich's new creative phase.[44]

For Grinberg, then, the old battles between Western decadence and "progressive" Soviet musical practice are over as far as Shostakovich is concerned: the composer has simply eliminated "constructivist" Western modernism from his creative palette. The victory of *Lady Macbeth* therefore becomes the vindication of Soviet cultural policy and Shostakovich's own successful absorption of both Russian classics and his own creative environment.

One of the most notable features of Soviet critical reactions to Shostakovich's updating of Leskov is the universal grasp of the composer's intentions, with several noting Leskov's own limited and "reactionary" social understanding. Georgii Polianovsky, reviewing the Nemirovich-Danchenko production (in Moscow called *Katerina Izmailova*) in February 1934, accused Leskov of "masking social truth" while Shostakovich exposes it:

> Leskov describes; Shostakovich exposes and reveals. Leskov is tendentiously pessimistic and calls for reconciliation, while Shostakovich . . . evokes hatred of the vile, accursed Leskovian

reality. . . . [H]e exposes the fundamental social oppression among the exploiters, the inertia, the exploitation barely covered by Christian humility.[45]

Polianovsky echoes Ostretsov's disapproval of the excessive "hopelessness" of Shostakovich's depiction of penal servitude ("The hopelessness and, most importantly, the absence, even in embryo, of positive characters and elements in the tragic depiction are the chief negative points of the opera) but does not hesitate to proclaim *Katerina Izmailova* "a truly landmark event in the history of Soviet musical theatre."[46]

The musicologist Evgeny Braudo was even warmer in his assessment, approvingly noting the influence of Meyerhold, though without giving examples from the staging:

We have before us the greatest achievement in Soviet musical drama in sixteen years. . . . Shostakovich has worked with the very best Soviet directors, especially Meyerhold, and this has certainly influenced his use of the most expressive devices from the Soviet theatrical stage. In "Katerina Izmailova" as in "The Nose," we see individual moments that have an unmistakably Meyerholdian imprint.[47]

The opening of a third production at the Bolshoi filial in November 1935 was significant in a number of ways. Although it was still essentially the Maly production with a different cast and conductor (because the Leningrad production was still running), the staging was slightly different in places, and several critics commented on this difference unfavorably. One particularly surprising detail to those who had seen the production in Leningrad was the central positioning of the bed in Act Two (and possibly also Act One), which in Leningrad had been more discreetly placed.[48] Another unfortunate detail, which may have particularly affected the performance on January 26 that Stalin attended, was that the box he habitually sat in—overhanging the right-hand side of the stage, not the old Tsar's box facing the stage—was positioned right over what was likely to have been (given traditions of opera pit layout) the brass section and the onstage brass band, which we know was used in this performance, including during the Act One sex scene, with its *fortissimo* brass parts.[49] Moreover, the orchestral parts for this performance contained a number of indications to play louder: the trombone glissandi that mark the culmination of the Act One sex scene were marked "all glissandi clearer [*iarche*]," while for the climax of the Passacaglia—the powerful, thickly scored orchestral interlude following Boris Timofeevich's death—the second horn and third trumpet parts were marked "pavillon en l'air" (with raised bells).[50] The effect must have been deafening. As Atovmian recalled, Shostakovich—who had watched the reactions in Stalin's box throughout from his box on the opposite side—was extremely distressed by the sonic assault on Stalin and his entourage, afterward asking his friend:

> Tell me, why was it necessary to increase the sonority of the "banda" so excessively? Those sitting in the government box must have been deafened by such a sonorous brass section. I feel in my heart that this year, like all leap years, will bring me another misfortune.[51]

We can only speculate on what might have been: Stalin would certainly have been deafened by the powerful brass, but it seems unlikely that he would have enjoyed *Lady Macbeth* even if he and Shostakovich had exchanged boxes. In all probability, it was simply not the kind of music that he liked, and Katerina was probably not the kind of heroine he liked either. Yet it is also probable that Stalin was less personally invested in Shostakovich's fall from grace than might be assumed. *Lady Macbeth* was, from this fateful evening, caught in a snare that was undoubtedly approved by Stalin, but which was executed and controlled by cultural officials eager for advancement, sustained by jealous or fearful musical colleagues and which, ultimately, claimed Meyerhold himself as its greatest prize: his theater was closed in 1938, the director was arrested in the summer of 1939 and shot in prison in 1940.[52]

THE WHEELS TURN

It seems there was never any firm consensus over who penned "Muddle instead of music" at the time of its publication. Though we know now that the author was Zaslavsky, and he was suspected by many of writing it even at the time, rumors over alternative authorships persisted, and Stalin himself was widely suspected of not only having authorized it but also possibly contributing to the text. In the now-discredited *Testimony*, Volkov's Shostakovich declared that

> There is a school of thought which holds that the article was written by the well-known bastard Zaslavsky. It might have been written down by the well-known bastard Zaslavsky, but that's another matter entirely. The article has too much of

Stalin in it, there are expressions that even Zaslavsky wouldn't have used, they were too ungrammatical. . . . I can distinguish with complete confidence Zaslavsky's bridges from Stalin's text.[53]

Although Volkov's Shostakovich was right about Zaslavsky, he was wrong about Stalin's editorial involvement. In a letter to Mattias Grinberg written in July 1953, Zaslavsky admits that he wrote the first of two articles about Shostakovich on instructions from above: "I would never have dared to write such an article. And all of a sudden, out of the blue, I got an assignment from top management. There were only two exact instructions: the title of the article 'Muddle instead of music' and the idea: music of this kind can lead to Meyerholdism.... I wrote the article right away, in one sitting, off the top of my head."[54] The text was apparently only lightly edited: "there were almost no editorial changes, only some minor stylistic ones." What is more, Zaslavsky claims that he intended the article to appear under his own name, not as a proxy for Stalin's own views: "I wrote that Shostakovich was a composer of outstanding talent and that he could correct his mistakes. The editor deleted this phrase. I don't know whether it was on his own initiative or on instructions from above. I objected strongly to this deletion and withdrew my signature. So the article turned out to be editorial and had a significance far in excess of what it would have had otherwise."[55]

Zaslavsky also offered this explanation as to why he would "not have dared" to criticize *Lady Macbeth* so vehemently before his commission:

Those articles ["Muddle" and "Balletic falsity"] were preceded by our [Zaslavsky's and Grinberg's] passionate discussions.[56] I recognized Shostakovich's exceptional talent. I liked some parts of *Katerina Izmailova*, but I did not accept this opera's musical agenda [*program*]. I rebelled against its musical principles. For me, it was a negation of opera. I could not, however, articulate my resistance. What I lacked was not so much musical education as courage. The authority of Shostakovich, and your own [Grinberg's] opinion, which I held in great respect, prevented my voicing it.[57]

That *Lady Macbeth* was almost untouchable by this time was something that only Stalin's personal support was able to overturn; Zaslavsky was merely the hired thug who enacted his displeasure. But once it was done, Zaslavsky's tirade emboldened other disgruntled figures in the music world to attack Shostakovich.

The cultural historian Leonid Maximenkov originally suspected the newly appointed chair of the Committee on Arts Affairs (*Komitet po delam iskusstv*), Platon Kerzhentsev, of writing "Muddle."[58] We now know he did not, although the musicologist Ekaterina Vlasova has speculated that Kerzhentsev may have commissioned Zaslavsky.[59] The formation of the KDI, which would oversee Soviet cultural life and report directly to the Politburo, was very recent, dating from January 1936, and Kerzhentsev had not yet stamped his authority on the cultural sphere over which he now assumed responsibility.

Maximenkov's sleuthing revealed that behind the scenes, two Central Committee officials, Alexander Shcherbakov and the musician-turned-bureaucrat Viktor Gorodinsky (the same Gorodinsky who had coauthored the Composers'

Union report with Iokhelson on *Lady Macbeth*), had contacted Stalin directly—bypassing Kerzhentsev—proposing awards and recognition for the achievements of Leningrad's Maly Theater at the expense of the allegedly hidebound Bolshoi. Shcherbakov was head of the Central Committee's department of culture and education, *Kultpros*, and Gorodinsky—Shostakovich's former Conservatoire classmate—was his assistant. They drew Stalin's attention to the work of the conductor Samuil Samosud in bringing two excellent new Soviet operas to the stage: Ivan Dzerzhinsky's new opera based on Mikhail Sholokhov's great civil war novel *The Quiet Don* (*Tikhii Don*) and Shostakovich's *Lady Macbeth*. They recommended honors and awards for several artists, including Samosud, and for across-the-board pay rises for Maly staff. Their plan was underpinned by a series of press articles emphasizing the Maly's leading role in developing Soviet theater and opera.[60]

As Maximenkov has shown, Stalin received the letter and swiftly authorized the pay raises. But to satisfy himself that these proposed honors were deserved, he went to see both operas for himself, which were then playing at the Bolshoi. As has already been documented, he enjoyed *The Quiet Don* and detested *Lady Macbeth*.[61] But it is unlikely that Kerzhentsev could actually have engineered this response from the outset. Even if he had in fact commissioned the article on Stalin's orders, he was surely an opportunist, not an instigator, at least of the initial attack on *Lady Macbeth*. The whole affair of "Muddle instead of music" was a perfect example of the behavior that the writer K. Dobronitsky described in the editorial's aftermath (as reported by an NKVD spy) thus: "If the higher-ups say 'a' then down below they recite the whole alphabet."[62] Anxiety to show oneself wholeheartedly in agreement with the latest political directive was already a key survival tactic of the Stalin era.

AFTER THE FALL

Attacks on Shostakovich, Sollertinsky, and *Lady Macbeth* in the aftermath of "Sumbur" have been well documented in English as well as in Russian.[63] Press correspondents attended meetings convened by the Composers' Union branches in Leningrad and Moscow in February 1936, and their reports can be found in *Pravda* and *Izvestiia*. A sample of the tone of proceedings can be gauged from *Pravda*'s report on the Leningrad discussion, noting the opera's defenders: "A. [Alexander] Rabinovich in vain attempted to illustrate the value of Shostakovich's opera Lady Macbeth"; Sollertinsky, described as a "notorious defender of bourgeois perversion in music," was deemed to have "still defended confusion, incomprehensibility and formalism in music." The report concluded, "Sollertinsky 'threatened' to cease his activity in music criticism, to which other participants . . . remarked, not without wit, that such a 'change of profession' for Sollertinsky would actually be a service." The final resolution agreed to reject "the uncritical apologists for bourgeois music of the contemporary West, which hindered the development of Soviet musical creativity in the style of socialist realism."[64] A few days later, the composer Ivan Dzerzhinsky reported for the paper *Izvestiia* on the Moscow discussions, where the pianist Heinrich Neuhaus actually told colleagues that he had left *Lady Macbeth* early, finding it boring, and complained that Shostakovich, unlike Leskov, who "wrote from the heart," displayed only cynicism, which, the pianist opined, "is unacceptable in art."[65] He quickly followed up his attack with an article for the Soviet arts press titled "On simplicity in art" (*O prostote v iskusstve*), comparing the work of contemporary Soviet composers unfavorably with those of the classics.[66]

Shortly after "Muddle" was published, Shostakovich asked his friend Isaak Glikman to subscribe to a newspaper-cutting service. The composer then collated all domestic and international articles in which he and his opera were mentioned from all over the Soviet Union and pasted them into three scrapbooks.[67] What is immediately striking about this press coverage is the absence of any further specific critique of *Lady Macbeth*. Those earlier, pre-"Muddle" criticisms advanced by Ostretsov, Bogdanov-Berezovsky, and others were not brought up again, because the entire debate was now in truth about something else, and discussions about music were taking place on the most generalized territory, stridently focused on rejecting Western influence. Zaslavsky's article had contained claims of laughable musical illiteracy: the reference to jazz in the opera, for instance, though likely prompted by the prominent trombone glissandi, was misplaced, and far from being cacophonous; critics had actually praised the opera for its beautiful and comprehensible music. Musicians knew this so were loath to make themselves ridiculous by repeating these claims. Instead, they signaled their loyalties in fairly generic terms according to their own principles and instincts. Eventually, even the most loyal among Shostakovich's friends—Sollertinsky included—voted in favor of the final resolution.[68]

Shostakovich continued collecting cuttings for the whole of 1936, and they show that the furor around *Lady Macbeth* died down very quickly. The reason for this, however, was not a happy one: the whirlwind passed swiftly from its first victim to others and turned into a wider cultural purge, culminating with Meyerhold's arrest in 1939. "Muddle instead of music" was followed up by an attack on Shostakovich's opera *The Limpid Stream*, and similar articles were published on other art forms, with further crude articles attacking "Daubing instead of painting" in children's books (*Maznia vmesto risunkov*), "Crude dogma instead of historical truth" (*Grubaia skhema vmesto istoricheskoi pravdy*) on the Ukrainian film *Prometheus*, and other hostile articles on the cultural sector more widely.[69] Shostakovich endured intense personal fear in the terrible purge year of 1937 (the year of his patron Tukhachevsky's arrest and execution and the arrests of Shostakovich's friend Levon Atovmian, his mother-in-law, and his sister Maria's husband).[70] He was permanently scarred by the trauma of what had happened to him, and his youthful confidence would never fully return.

CHAPTER 2

FROM "PORNOPHONY" TO MASTERPIECE

HOW THE WEST WAS WON

I N THE LAST CHAPTER, we saw how *Lady Macbeth* was understood by Shostakovich's contemporaries at the time of its composition and triumphal reception in Soviet Russia. Here, we look at the painful episode of *Pravda*'s critique in January 1936 and at Shostakovich's revision of the opera in the 1950s, with a major cut to the Act One sex scene. We then examine the second life of *Lady Macbeth* following Rostropovich's EMI recording, released in 1979, and the subsequent publication of the revised "original" score by Hans Sikorski.

As we saw in the introduction, Rostropovich's timing in releasing his bombshell recording could hardly have been better, coinciding as it did with the publication of Solomon Volkov's sensationalist *Testimony*. In a remarkably short

Shostakovich's Lady Macbeth of the Mtsensk District. Pauline Fairclough, Oxford University Press.
© Oxford University Press 2025. DOI: 10.1093/9780197534977.003.0002

space of time, both *Testimony* and *Lady Macbeth* had joined forces to stun audiences and readers worldwide. Critics, music writers, conductors, and opera houses now perceived *Lady Macbeth* as the pinnacle of Shostakovich's unadulterated genius, written before Stalin's interference in his career. Performances of *Lady Macbeth* in the 1980s became box office sensations, and *Katerina Izmailova* quickly all but vanished from Western opera houses.[1]

On the face of it, *Lady Macbeth*'s restoration might seem like natural justice. But its revival story is complicated by the fact that *Katerina Izmailova* was Shostakovich's own revision, made of his own free will in the more liberal post-Stalin era, and with the generous assistance of his close friend Isaak Glikman, who revised the libretto at the composer's request. Although *Katerina Izmailova* is regularly assumed to be a "sanitized" version that we can honorably ignore today, in fact, as we will see, all the available evidence points to the fact that it remained Shostakovich's preferred version. He refused to authorize revivals of *Lady Macbeth* once his revision was available for hire internationally, and his letters to Glikman show a clear desire to remove the most vulgar language. Indeed, Shostakovich's complete autograph score of *Lady Macbeth*—one of his most treasured possessions, taken with him when he was evacuated from Leningrad during the Nazi blockade in 1942—bears witness to the composer's determination to replace *Lady Macbeth* with *Katerina Izmailova* in a particularly decisive way.[2] The biggest change was the wholesale excision of the Act One sex scene between Katerina and the worker Sergei. Shostakovich removed over one hundred bars of the opera's most powerful music, either pasting replacement pages over them so firmly that his original score could no longer be accessed or crossing out the music with thick red pencil.[3]

We now turn to *Lady Macbeth*'s premature demise on the personal orders of Joseph Stalin, who went to see the opera at the Bolshoi's filial stage on January 26, 1936, and left before the end (how much of the opera he heard has never been established, but he was there at least for Acts One and Two; it seems likely that he missed Act Four entirely). Two days later, an unsigned editorial appeared in the Soviet newspaper *Pravda* titled "Muddle instead of music" (*Sumbur vmesto muzyki*) in which Shostakovich was accused of writing music that was incomprehensible and cacophonous:

> From the first minute, the listener is shocked by deliberate dissonance, by a confused stream of sound. Snatches of melody, the beginnings of a musical phrase, are drowned, emerge again, and disappear in a grinding and squealing roar. To follow this "music" is most difficult; to remember it, impossible.[4]

As a critique of the musical language of *Lady Macbeth*, the editorial suggests the response of someone who disliked contemporary music and had simply found the opera too difficult to follow. But worse followed:

> The composer of Lady Macbeth was forced to borrow from jazz its nervous, convulsive, and spasmodic music in order to lend "passion" to his characters. While our critics, including music critics, swear by the name of socialist realism, the stage serves us, in Shostakovich's creation, the coarsest kind of naturalism. He reveals the merchants and the people monotonously and bestially. The predatory merchant woman who scrambles into

the possession of wealth through murder is pictured as some kind of "victim" of bourgeois society. Leskov's story has been given a significance which it does not possess.

And all this is coarse, primitive and vulgar. The music quacks, grunts, and growls, and suffocates itself in order to express the love scenes as naturalistically as possible. And "love" is smeared all over the opera in the most vulgar manner. The merchant's double bed occupies the central position on the stage. On this bed all "problems" are solved. In the same coarse, naturalistic style is shown the death from poisoning and the flogging—both practically on stage.[5]

Pravda was the official Communist Party newspaper, so an unsigned article printed there carried obvious editorial authority. *Lady Macbeth* had been a huge success since it had opened in January 1934 in both Leningrad and Moscow, praised by every single music critic who had reviewed it. A change of tone of this magnitude could not have happened without sanction from the very top. Shostakovich had already been anxious about the chance of Politburo members, or even Stalin himself, coming to see his opera.[6] The tenor Sergei Radamsky, who sat with Shostakovich that fateful night, left us this account of the composer's state of mind:

Stalin, Mikoyan and Zhdanov sat in the Government box, which was over the orchestra pit, directly over the percussion and brass sections. Shostakovich, Meyerhold and Achmateli (head of the Tiflis theater) and myself (as Shostakovich's guests) sat in the box opposite. We could see the occupants of the Government box clearly, except for Stalin, who sat behind a narrow curtain. . . . Every time the percussion and brasses let loose in full forte, we noticed that Zhdanov and Mikoyan jumped and turned to Stalin with hilarity. . . . Shostakovich, having seen how the three were laughing and amusing themselves, hid at the rear of our box and covered his face with his hands. His nervousness was so extreme that his face was running with perspiration.[7]

Radamsky went on to recall that the critic from *Izvestiia* had allegedly asked Stalin how he had liked the opera and received the reply "this is muddle, not music" (*eto sumbur, a ne muzyka*). Whether or not this is true will probably never be known, although we do now know who wrote the article. As many suspected at the time, it was written by a *Pravda* staff journalist called David Zaslavsky, but to order: by his own admission, he would never have written anything so negative without the highest authority.[8] The Bolshoi performance ran twice more (January 29 and February 3), and its final scheduled performance on February 10 was then cancelled, advertised as "due to artist illness."[9]

Zaslavsky's article was devastating, not just for Shostakovich but also for many of the best artists working in the Soviet Union, as ripples from its initial impact gradually spread through Soviet cultural life. It is worth summarizing Zaslavsky's specific points: First, he makes a disapproving allusion to jazz (based on the trombone slides that accompany the Act One sex scene as well as signaling other sexually focused activities or innuendos in Act One), which to Zaslavsky's mind evoked a generalized "decadent" Western music. Second, he criticized the "coarse naturalism" of the opera. Third, the entire premise of Shostakovich's adaptation of Nikolai Leskov's 1865 novella *Lady Macbeth of the Mtsensk District*—intended to reframe the story from a modern Soviet perspective, using familiar Soviet techniques of political satire and critique—is explicitly rejected.

Although the Bolshoi run was cut short by one performance, the opera continued to play at the two main theaters where it had been running since January 1934: Moscow's Nemirovich-Danchenko Theater and Leningrad's Maly Theater.[10] Nemirovich-Danchenko's production ran under the title *Katerina Izmailova*, and since the director himself averred that the main fault with the Bolshoi's performance had been Alexander Melik-Pashaev's overeager conducting, he allowed it to continue to run in his theater until he was pressured to stop.[11] Incredibly, Nemirovich-Danchenko's production continued until March 7, the final performance deliberately scheduled to celebrate International Women's Day (March 8).[12] But after that, *Lady Macbeth* would not be heard again in Russia, not just in Stalin's lifetime or in Shostakovich's lifetime, but for the duration of the Soviet Union itself. Audiences in Russia heard Shostakovich's original score again only in 1996 and 1997, in concert performances in St. Petersburg and at the Moscow Conservatory Great Hall, conducted by Rostropovich. Although *Lady Macbeth* is still sometimes performed in Russia today, the flagship national opera house, the Moscow Bolshoi, has staged *Lady Macbeth* (original version) only once since 1936 (in 2004), despite holding all the original orchestral parts from 1935.[13]

Shostakovich first contemplated a revival of *Lady Macbeth* after Stalin's death in 1953 and then the passing of his wife, Nina, the following year. He asked his close friend Isaak Glikman to carry out changes to the libretto, in some cases being very specific about the textual alterations, particularly eliminating coarse language and downplaying the "idea of the insatiable female."[14] But he also authorized Glikman to go through the whole libretto and make changes that he felt were necessary.[15] Once he had received Glikman's work, Shostakovich wrote to thank him and voiced the opinion that he wished he had asked him to do it twenty-two years ago.[16] But even after these changes were made, *Lady Macbeth* was still not passed for performance: after the minister for culture Viacheslav Molotov formed a special committee to examine the revised opera in 1956, it was subjected to the same barrage of criticism it had received following the publication of the *Pravda* editorial in 1936.[17] It was only after Shostakovich had been pressured into joining the Communist Party in 1960 that the chairman of the Soviet Composers' Union, Tikhon Khrennikov, arranged for it to be performed. Under its new title, *Katerina Izmailova*, and with a new opus number (op. 114), finally on January 8, 1963, *Lady Macbeth* was once again performed on the Soviet stage: the Stanislavsky-Nemirovich-Danchenko Theater in Moscow.[18] Shostakovich embarked on a tour in 1963–64 to attend productions of *Katerina Izmailova* in Riga, London, Zagreb, Vienna, Kazan, Kiev, Ruse (Bulgaria), Leningrad, and Budapest. From this moment on Shostakovich would never sanction a performance of the original *Lady Macbeth*, despite a request from La Scala in 1964.[19]

FROM KATERINA ON FILM TO LADY MACBETH'S REVIVAL

In 1965, Shostakovich collaborated closely with the director Mikhail Shapiro on the Leningrad film studio (Lenfilm) production of the full opera *Katerina Izmailova*, with Galina Vishnevskaya in the title role. And though Vishnevskaya wrote ironically about the filming process—recalling how the actor playing Sergei (Artem Inozemtsev) had been forced to shave his chest ("We are making a film for the laboring masses, not for sex maniacs!")—in fact, the film was warmly received by Soviet critics, and Vishnevskaya played a transformative role in the next chapter of this opera's beleaguered history.[20] Through working with Vishnevskaya for Shapiro's film, Shostakovich discovered that she was able and willing to sing the high tessitura of Katerina's role in places where all previous singers in the 1930s had refused, afraid of damaging their voices. He had copied his original vocal lines into Vishnevskaya's part, hoping that she would fulfill his original intention. When she performed for him—not without anxieties of her own—Shostakovich was elated: "Galya . . . much of what you sang just now I have never heard before. . . . When I wrote it, all the sopranos refused to sing it. . . . So I had to rewrite the vocal part."[21]

It may well have been this revelation, as well as his close friendship with both her and Rostropovich, that inspired Shostakovich to allow parts of the original score of *Lady Macbeth* to be performed by his friends. Rostropovich conducted the orchestral entr'actes in Gorky (present-day Nizhni Novgorod) in 1962.[22] But we should note that Shostakovich's firm refusal to La Scala to perform *Lady Macbeth* came as late as 1964: he insisted that they either perform *Katerina Izmailova* or leave his opera alone.[23] Therefore, even hearing Vishnevskaya perform did not persuade Shostakovich to allow a revival of *Lady Macbeth* in its entirety. If we trust his letters to Glikman, Shostakovich believed that the changes he had made to the opera were for the better. Changes to tessitura could be reversed, but there is no evidence to suggest that his textual changes, his new entr'acte, and the excision of the sex scene were equally dispensable. Glikman asserted that Shostakovich, far from being "forced" to clean up parts of the libretto, did so of his own free will: "The truth is that when the opera was originally performed . . . the inappropriate reaction of some members of the audience to the rumbustious, vulgar and iconoclastic remarks made by Sergey and some of the other characters upset Shostakovich."[24] Moreover, getting *Katerina Izmailova* to the stage had been a drawn-out, painful, and arduous undertaking, likely making Shostakovich all the more committed to the new version. A reversal might also have been embarrassing for him both personally and politically. International memories of the Act One sex scene had faded to the extent that remarkably few critics attending the premiere of *Katerina Izmailova*, including some who had actually heard *Lady Macbeth* in the 1930s, noticed that the scene had been cut. The revised opera was advertised as more or less the same as *Lady Macbeth*, but with some minor musical and textual changes. A forceful reminder in Europe of just what Shostakovich had actually cut from *Lady Macbeth* was, we might infer, the last thing the composer wanted. Outside the Communist bloc, gleeful accusations of sanitization for political reasons would have been inevitable.

Thereafter, the saga of how Rostropovich came to record *Lady Macbeth* for EMI in 1978 and present a 1932 copyist's score to the German publishing house Hans Sikorski in 1979 grows murky. Rostropovich was forced to leave the Soviet Union for political reasons in 1974, shortly followed by Vishnevskaya and their two daughters. Fueled by Cold War sensationalism, a rumor started in 1980 that Rostropovich had "smuggled the score into the West."[25] In the New Collected Works orchestral score of *Lady Macbeth*, the editor Irina Levasheva reported that Irina Shostakovich, the composer's third wife, gave the score to Rostropovich for his recording in the second half of the 1970s—though given that Rostropovich was by then living outside the Soviet Union, this seems unlikely.[26] The introduction to the Sikorski score merely states that Rostropovich "rediscovered" it, but when EMI re-released their original recording on CD in 2002, the author of the liner note, Richard Osborne, claimed that Rostropovich had found the score in Dimitri Mitropoulos's archive in the Library of Congress, adding that Shostakovich had personally asked Rostropovich to conduct the original version of *Lady Macbeth* in the West.[27] Finding the score in the Library of Congress was also the account given by the EMI sound engineer Suvi Raj Grubb, who published his memoir in 1986, seeming to confirm this account conclusively.[28]

But Grubb also adds that Rostropovich additionally used another source, which he never revealed. And of course, this is the critical issue, because the vocal score in the Mitropoulos archive (one of the glass print copies made for the Nemirovich-Danchenko Theater in 1933), like the published Muzgiz vocal score of 1935, omits the postcoital trombone slides and has other cuts and textual variants that Rostropovich rejected in his search for the "unexpurgated" version that he knew existed somewhere. Grubb tells us that EMI staff attempted to source this version for Rostropovich themselves but found that every opera house that had performed *Lady Macbeth* in the 1930s had returned the orchestral score.[29] However the score came to Rostropovich, obtaining it in time to make the EMI recording was a fraught experience. As Rostropovich described in a letter to the Sikorski agent Jürgen Köchel, "You can't imagine the difficulties I had obtaining the score for the first edition of 'Lady Macbeth'. . . . I obtained the score only three weeks before the scheduled recording and therefore had to hire many copyists to do the orchestra parts in that short time."[30]

To my mind, the most plausible account comes from Larisa Chirkova, archivist at Rostropovich's museum-flat in St. Petersburg, who knew Rostropovich well. According to her, Rostropovich obtained his copy of the orchestral score from Universal Edition in Vienna thanks to the émigré Soviet composer Mikhail Goldstein who located it there, and this remains the most likely scenario: in the 1930s, the Soviet music publisher Muzgiz and Universal Edition had a copublishing relationship, making Vienna a natural home for a copy of the score.[31]

The idea that Shostakovich sanctioned (let alone requested) the revival of *Lady Macbeth* in the West remains unverified. Vishnevskaya does not make any such claim in her memoir, nor did Rostropovich when he performed *Lady Macbeth* in Russia (despite giving multiple press interviews).[32] Given the closeness and trust between Rostropovich and Shostakovich, it is hard to believe that Rostropovich deliberately went against the composer's stated wishes, and it is always possible that Shostakovich did privately make this request to him. Or, perhaps more likely, Rostropovich felt sure that Shostakovich, in his heart, would have wanted him to conduct *Lady Macbeth* in the West, and he was prepared to go to extraordinary lengths—not to mention considerable expense and effort—to make that happen.[33]

Whatever the truth, *Lady Macbeth*'s popularity since EMI released Rostropovich's recording in 1979 has been remarkable. Only a few performances of *Katerina Izmailova* outside Russia have been produced since, while *Lady Macbeth* is a regular fixture in international opera houses. Within just the 2022–23 season there have been at least three revivals of major productions: the New York Metropolitan Opera (Graham Vick, 1994), the Grand Théâtre de Genève (Calixto Bieito, 2014), and the Vienna State Opera (Matthias Hartmann, 2009), as well as a new production at the Staatsoper Hamburg (Angelina Nikonova, 2023). Whether or not he could have predicted it, Rostropovich launched a new classic on the opera stage; without his EMI recording, *Lady Macbeth* might never have been revived at all.

LADY MACBETH *AND THE COLD WAR MARKETPLACE*

Yet the success of *Lady Macbeth* was not a foregone conclusion, even allowing for the brilliance of the EMI recording and Vishnevskaya's extraordinary rendering of the title role. As already noted, its release in 1979 coincided with the publication of Solomon Volkov's *Testimony*. Painting Shostakovich as a closet dissident, the book caused an international sensation, overturning decades of Western assumptions about Shostakovich as a dutiful Communist composer and making his music even more popular in the West.[34] Musicians who had known Shostakovich were grilled on their opinion of *Testimony*, Rostropovich among them.[35] Understandably, some of Shostakovich's friends, keen to burnish Shostakovich's Western reputation as an anti-Stalinist, endorsed the book's authenticity without worrying too much about Volkov's more exaggerated (and subsequently discredited) claims to have captured every word of *Testimony* directly from interviews with the composer. By commissioning Volkov to write the sleeve note accompanying his recording, EMI cleverly harnessed these two potent phenomena, and the world's music media was not slow to take up the cue. In this charged environment, Volkov's claim for the authenticity of *Lady Macbeth* had a powerful impact, read by every press reviewer and recycled in program notes in the international performances that followed. As Volkov claimed regarding the preparation of *Katerina Izmailova*, "The changes in music and in the text of the libretto were obviously made under the pressure of circumstances," while Rostropovich's recording "restores historic and aesthetic justice to one of the most brilliant compositions of modern Russian music."[36] The framework for *Lady Macbeth*'s canonization and *Katerina Izmailova*'s rejection was thus set in place, and the stage set for *Lady Macbeth*'s conquering of the world's operatic stages.

CHAPTER 3

STAGING SEX
IN THE 1930S

WHAT THE LIBRETTO TELLS US

A S WE HAVE SEEN in the previous chapter, it was not the sex in *Lady Macbeth* that brought controversy down on Shostakovich's head. Rather, it was a combination of changing ideological positions, jostling for power among arts bureaucrats, and a history of hostility between parts of the Moscow and Leningrad musical "establishment" and Shostakovich's close friend Ivan Sollertinsky that poisoned the critical debates around the opera in 1936. Indeed, it was only during these debates that the opera's sexual content was raised at all as a matter of controversy—an entirely new criticism of the formerly much-praised opera.

Yet the opera's sexual content has loomed large in its reception since Rostropovich's revival in 1979. As noted in chapter 2, a major ingredient of Rostropovich's revival

Shostakovich's Lady Macbeth of the Mtsensk District. Pauline Fairclough, Oxford University Press.
© Oxford University Press 2025. DOI: 10.1093/9780197534977.003.0003

of *Lady Macbeth* was the replacement of the excised sex scene. And to justify that, the narrative that the composer's creative decisions in the 1950s were forced upon him because of Soviet ideology became essential. Instances of absurd prudishness during the filming of *Katerina Izmailova* for Lenfilm were, as we saw in chapter 2, amusingly highlighted by Galina Vishnevskaya in her autobiography. But where the staged opera was concerned, Rostropovich only really had his personal conviction that *Lady Macbeth* was superior to *Katerina Izmailova* as his basis for scouring Europe and the US for that copyist score he passionately wanted to find: the one with all the trombone glissandi kept in. It is worth stressing again that, with the Nemirovich-Danchenko glass-print copy he found in the Library of Congress, Rostropovich had a perfectly adequate basis for a "revival" recording of *Lady Macbeth*. But he did not stop searching until the unexpurgated version had been found. Following Rostropovich's lead, opera directors now universally choose *Lady Macbeth* over *Katerina Izmailova*, and because of the opera's history of persecution, the shocking nature of the sex scene has become conflated with its banishment in a way that renders it difficult to criticize. This chapter and the next therefore look in detail at the creation and reception history of this key scene, as well as the preceding scene of sexual assault (of the housekeeper Aksinya), as a way of peeling back the layers of mythology that, I believe, prevent us from seeing these scenes more clearly and being able to critique them or take strong directorial decisions around them.

LADY MACBETH'S *SEXUAL POLITICS THEN AND NOW*

The two scenes of sexual violence in Act One of *Lady Macbeth* lie at the heart of what makes the original opera so troubling to listeners informed by twenty-first-century sexual ethics (as anyone who has taught this opera to students in recent years can confirm). We have noted already that neither scene seems to have troubled contemporary audiences in the 1930s. But it is the second of these scenes in particular—the famous sex scene between Katerina and the worker Sergei—which is today most controversial, because the sex between them is clearly nonconsensual as far as the libretto is concerned, yet the scene concludes with Katerina's adoring declaration "I have no husband, only you alone." Most contemporary directors work around the stark anomalies with great ingenuity, with the result that the awkward issue of nonconsent (Katerina crying out, "Let go!," "I'm frightened," and "I don't wa. . . ") is successfully glossed over in live production. However, even in Shostakovich's lifetime, listening to operas via recorded performance became commonplace, and here the dramatic problems of this scene are laid bare.

Evidence that Shostakovich was uneasy from very early on about how to frame the sex scene between Katerina and Sergei can be discerned from the multiple changes of heart he had—either from his own reflections or from discussions with the directors and conductors he worked with: Smolich and Samosud at the Maly, Mordvinov and Grigori Stoliarov at the Nemirovich-Danchenko. It is of course impossible to tease apart which decisions came from the composer and which from a director or conductor. But the fact that the older Shostakovich was not prepared to include this scene in *Katerina Izmailova* is surely revealing in itself.

The musicologist Laurel Fay has shown that multiple changes to the postcoital dialogue in manuscript sources from the 1930s record indecision both here and in other parts of the Act One libretto that relate to Katerina's sexual longing. Since Fay has published extensive details of this scene's source discrepancies and revisions, I will only briefly summarize her findings below. However, since Fay's findings in 1994, the New Collected Works score of *Lady Macbeth* was published, containing not only Manashir Yakubov's research on the libretto but also a valuable facsimile of the early draft score with Shostakovich's marginalia and those of the Maly conductor Samuil Samosud. These notes show that changes made in this score may well reflect decisions taken during rehearsal for that production.[1] We will examine these in detail later in this chapter and in chapter 4, where we will address both scenes of sexual assault in *Lady Macbeth*. To contextualize this part of the opera, we will also consider the contemporary presentation of sexual violence in Soviet literature and theater in the late 1920s to early 1930s and its roots in real-life events.

KATERINA'S ARIA

When preparing his version of *Lady Macbeth* for the EMI recording, Rostropovich—working from both the Nemirovich-Danchenko glass print and his newly acquired unnamed source—changed the text of Katerina's Act One aria in accordance with that source. In both the 1933

Nemirovich-Danchenko and 1935 published Muzgiz scores, Katerina sings this text: "Once I saw from my window a little nest/Two birds were sitting there/A dove with her mate/I often look at them/And weep from envy/I myself have no dear one [*golubka*]/I have no freedom and I cannot fly/I have no darling mate." As Fay has documented, though, manuscript sources from the 1930s show that there were actually two versions of this aria text, and Shostakovich seems to have changed his mind several times about which to use. In the program booklet (which includes a full libretto) for the Nemirovich-Danchenko production, the text is different: "The young colt runs to the filly/the tomcat seeks the female/the dove flies to its mate/but no one comes to me. The breeze caresses the birch-tree/the sun shines and warms it./There is someone to smile upon everyone/but no one comes to me./No one will put his arm around my waist/no one will press his lips to mine/no one will stroke my white breast/no one will exhaust me with his caresses." This text is reproduced in the Sikorski score, but for *Katerina Izmailova*, Shostakovich restored the "little nest" text, with a slight variation at the end: instead of "I have no freedom and I cannot fly/I have no darling mate," Katerina sings, "An eternity without love/an eternity locked up/akh, no freedom, no will."[2] The less suggestive aria text was not created for *Katerina Izmailova* in the 1950s but was written more or less at the same time as the more sexually explicit one.

The New Collected Works facsimile of the earlier opera draft, with Act One clearly dated in Shostakovich's hand (October 30, 1931), shows that Shostakovich's original text was the colt/filly version. However, at some point,

Shostakovich wrote in the alternative, less suggestive, text above it.[3] The production notes from director Nikolai Smolich (kept by his assistant N. Shulgin) show that the "little nest" text was sung in Leningrad.[4] Shostakovich also chose the "little nest" version for his authorized Muzgiz score in 1935, a decision he held to when making his later revisions in the 1950s. The two copyist orchestral scores from the 1930s donated by Levon Atovmian and now held at the Russian Museum of Musical Culture do not offer any decisive clarification on the decision-making process. Both contain the "colt/filly" text (with some additional pairs of mating animals listed), but one of them also has the "little nest" text added above the stave, rather faintly, in pencil.[5] As Irina Levasheva has noted, this score is a copy of the other and bears markings of the Bolshoi Theater library as well as the conductor's markings (by Bolshoi conductor Alexander Melik-Pashaev) from the time of the 1935–36 production, with some further corrections by Shostakovich, plus a note to say that he had read and checked it. This being so, it shows us that the "little nest" text was at least considered for the Bolshoi production and was possibly used in preference to the "colt/filly" version.

THE TROMBONE GLISSANDI AND AFTER

One of the most deliberately outrageous moments in *Lady Macbeth* is the moment where, immediately after the violent music accompanying the sex scene has ended, a drawn-out trombone glissando from b flat to g (marked *fff*) signals Sergei's withdrawal from Katerina. Seven bars later, now at a slower tempo (*Andante*) and *piano*, three further *glissandi* repeat a short fall from f to e over quiet tremolo strings. The effect is obviously comic, and in modern-day productions, audiences invariably chuckle at this moment. But given the seriousness of the scene—emphatically not intended as comic overall—Shostakovich vacillated over whether to retain the *glissandi.* His uncertainty probably stemmed from ambiguity in the libretto immediately afterward, for some of the most problematic text in the Act One sex scene concerns what Katerina and Sergei say to each other after sex. Throughout Sergei's assault on her, the music has been that of a violent chase—as indicated in Smolich's stage notes for the Leningrad production: "A silent struggle. Sergei drags Katerina behind the curtain but she escapes and runs to the door; Sergei will not let her go and again there is a struggle. Katerina runs to the window, but Sergei grabs her; she runs to the dressing-table and falls. Sergei picks her up, embraces her tightly and carries her behind the curtain." In the sources containing all the music originally written for this scene, the violent "chase" music characterized by sharp offbeat upward trombone thrusts gives way to the *fff* solo trombone slides described above and then to the three short *glissandi.* After a bar's pause, Katerina enters, unac-companied, with two simple four-bar phrases, very low in her range (middle c' to a' flat, then d' to f'). Though her words were altered in different versions of the early score, her music remains unchanged: it is subdued and fragmen-tary, denoting exhaustion. As Fay has noted, the dialogue at this point caused Shostakovich problems early on, and the draft score facsimile published later confirms this, since it is dated 1931—although of course we don't know when the extra text was added. In the Nemirovich-Danchenko print of 1933, two whole rehearsal figures are cut here: R191 (the three short descending "postclimactic" trombone *glissandi*) and R193 (Sergei's gloating "ho ho" speech, discussed further below), and these are also cut in the Muzgiz 1935 score, which Shostakovich personally prepared for publication. Rostropovich, when making his EMI recording, also cut R193 from his new source—many conductors still do—but restored the three suggestive trombone glissandi at R191. The two copyist scores in the Russian Museum of Musical Culture both erase R193 (Sergei's gloating), which is crossed out in pencil, but retain all of the trombone *glissandi*.

That Shostakovich cooled toward this cheeky sound effect, however, is confirmed both by the draft facsimile of 1931 and by a report Sergei Radamsky sent to the *New York Times* in which he stated that the trombone *glissandi* were cut altogether in the Nemirovich-Danchenko production and "very much subdued" in the Maly.[6] However, Smolich's stage directions suggest that Radamsky's memory of the Leningrad production may have been at fault here, since the documentary evidence points to them being cut altogether. The 1931 draft facsimile shows that Shostakovich actually scratched the three postcoital *glissandi* (R191) out of the score, while the longer *glissando* immediately beforehand (R190) has also been lightly crossed out. Their excision in the draft facsimile begs the question of whether they were performed in Leningrad at all. From Shulgin's notes, prepared from Smolich's rehearsals, it seems that the whole section from R191 to Boris's call to Katerina at R195 was cut completely in Leningrad—in other words, there may have been no *glissandi* and no postcoital dialogue in this production at all.[7]

As Glikman tells us, Shostakovich was upset by audience laughter in places he felt were inappropriate, and today these trombone slides often provoke giggles at a point where the drama of the scene is at a point of high tension.[8] It may even be the case that the only contemporary Soviet production to have included all of them was the Bolshoi filial staging that Stalin saw. As we saw in the previous chapter, Melik-Pashaev actually instructed his trombones to play the *glissandi* "more clearly" (*iarche*) and the parts themselves—preserved in the Bolshoi Theater to this day, and which I was able to view in 2019—are marked *ffff* for the initial "big" *glissando* at R190.[9] The effect would have been overwhelming for Stalin and his entourage, seated as they were over the brass section.

PROBLEMS OF TEXT

If the trombone slides caused Shostakovich to waver, then the postcoital dialogue between Sergei and Katerina provoked even more indecisiveness. This is not surprising given the impossible brief that he and Preis had set themselves. What was a rather rough-and-ready seduction scene in Leskov was to become an assault in the opera, yet the end result must remain the same: Katerina has to fall in love with Sergei. And this transformation from terrified woman to satiated lover must take place within the span of a few minutes. As I believe Shostakovich came to realize, there was almost no version of their dialogue that could overcome this anomaly; the radical nature of the changes he made for the Moscow and Leningrad productions bears witness to his struggle to overcome it.

What immediately follows the sex scene in the libretto seems to have been jumbled from the outset and differs in every source. I will begin with the Sikorski version, since that is the one that most readers will know. After the sex is over, and we hear Katerina sing her subdued, unaccompanied lines "Now go, for god's sake/I am a married woman" (Sikorski, R192), Sergei immediately laughs, singing, "Ho ho! I've never seen a married woman give herself to me so quickly," ending a prolonged gloat with an incongruous "Let's not speak of it." Katerina's response to this is simply "I have no husband, only you alone" and, after a brief interpolation by Boris Timofeevich and Sergei's refusal to leave, she declares her love for him in the last word of the scene: "Darling!"[10] Minus the gloating in R193, this is the version popularized by Rostropovich's EMI recording, and (plus or minus the gloating) which we generally hear in opera houses today.

We don't know whether either Sergei's gloating or Katerina's "Darling" were ever performed in Leningrad and Moscow in the 1930s. Both the "Darling!" and Sergei's "ho ho" outburst at R193 are included in the two copyist scores held in the Russian Museum of Musical Culture, although one of these has Sergei's "ho ho"—the whole of R193—crossed out.[11] They are also present in the other copyist score that Rostropovich obtained. If we take the 1931 draft facsimile score as representative of what changes Samosud and Shostakovich may have made in rehearsals, we see that Shostakovich changed his mind about the awkward dialogue when preparing for the Maly production.

Until this point, looking only at the copyist and published scores, this crucial postcoital dialogue, though undergoing changes, could plausibly indicate Katerina's emotional capitulation, even sexual exhaustion: the fragmentary intonation of her short, low-pitched phrases suit that interpretation as well as any other. However, in the 1931 draft score, a critical change was made that forces us to consider a darker interpretation. Shostakovich's original underlay has Katerina singing, "Why did you do that? I am a married woman" (*Zachem ty sdelal eto/Ia muzhniaia zhena*), but Shostakovich has crossed this out and replaced it with "Don't you dare touch me/I am a married woman" (*Ne smei menia kasatsia*), making it abundantly clear that her mood at this moment is a negative one. Sergei's response too is altered in this draft score. In the 1931 draft, Shostakovich used the text "Ho ho! I've never seen a married woman soil the bed with blood/Ho ho, Zinovii, ho, Borisich, ho ho ho, he couldn't. . . . Ho ho (etc)" (*Kho kho! Shto-to ne videl ia muzhnie zheny postel' krov'iu* [illegible]/*Kho, Zinovii, kho, Borisich, kho kho kho, zhenu ne smog. . . . Kho kho* [etc.]).[12] The line "Let's not speak of that," ultimately given to Sergei in later published sources, was here originally sung by Katerina, in response to this crude outburst. But Shostakovich then crossed out the whole speech, indicating that the scene should proceed straight from Katerina's "Don't you dare touch me/I am a married woman" to "Let's not speak of that." Once he had eradicated Sergei's uncouth gloating, it made no sense to give this phrase to Katerina, and so Sergei ended up singing "Let's not speak of that," now in response to "I am a married woman." Such a change directs us away from a more casual understanding of the words that were finally printed in Shostakovich's authorized 1935 Muzgiz score: "Why, why

Seryozha?" Even if the textual change to "Don't you dare touch me" (which he did not retain in the 1935 score, nor in any other manuscript source) was not Shostakovich's idea, the reasoning behind it was surely to remove any ambiguity in Katerina's emotional state. We are to understand that she is upset, not enamored. Shostakovich did not keep this text in any of the later versions of the score from the 1930s, including the published Muzgiz score of 1935, but the true mood of this dramatic moment is, I believe, unchanged from his original conception.

Shostakovich also vacillated over the next line in the draft, originally Katerina's "I have no husband/only you alone," which he crossed out and replaced with "No, I am afraid of my husband, let go of me Sergei" (*Net, ia boius' muzha, otpusti Sergei*). Katerina's final cry "Darling!" (*Milyi!*) at the very end is present in this draft but was removed in the Nemirovich-Danchenko score, which signs off vocally with Sergei's "Come, Katya!" (*A nu, Katia!*). When preparing the score for publication by Muzgiz in 1935, Shostakovich did not restore "Darling!," settling on the alteration he had made in the Nemirovich-Danchenko score for both published sources.[13] Both Nemirovich-Danchenko and Muzgiz scores cut Sergei's gloating, and in both, Katerina's line "I am afraid of my husband" is changed back to "Now I have no husband/only you alone." Again, the vacillation seems to have been caused by uncertainty over how willing Katerina should appear to be: should she be a clear victim of rape, or should she say "no" while meaning "yes"? The latter suggestion, however distasteful to twenty-first-century sexual ethics, was uncontroversial in Shostakovich's time, as the lack of comment in contemporary reviews makes clear. Yet these apparently minor textual changes pull us back to a darker interpretation: even in 1931, decisions were taken to suggest that Katerina is a victim of sexual assault and rape. Her "no" meant "no," but Shostakovich and Preis felt that a rapid change of heart afterward could still be plausible, which—especially given audience knowledge of Leskov's text—was a fair assumption in the 1930s.[14]

The question of whether to emphasize Katerina's virginity, referring to the inaccurate belief that all virgins bleed on penetration, is addressed by Manashir Yakubov's essay on the libretto. As Yakubov shows, Preis's original libretto ran as follows:

SERGEI: My joy!
EKATERINA: What for? I am a married woman.
SERGEI: Married? I've never seen married women soil the bed with blood! Have you really been a virgin all this time? So if not me . . . ?
EKATERINA: Don't talk about it. My darling! I don't have a husband, you are my one and only, Sergei! Do it again . . . .
SERGEI: Aha! You've taken a fancy to it![15]

As we have seen, a version of this dialogue was in Shostakovich's first draft, although he discarded it, and in at least one source (the copyist score used by Rostropovich and Sikorski) he replaced the reference to blood with prolonging Sergei's gloating over Zinovy and mocking Katerina for her eagerness. But aside from that, although unpleasantly graphic, Preis's dialogue makes logical sense. Although Katerina still undergoes what seems like a sudden change of heart, it is not quite as incongruous as that found in any of the printed scores. In stripping back Preis's lines, Shostakovich wisely removed verbiage that was both naïve and distasteful but seems not to have realized that what was left—in any of the versions—lacked dramatic credibility. The leap from Katerina's "Now go" to "Darling!" is nonsensical, if we look only at the score. Only careful staging that would show Katerina and Sergei as lovers—showing that the rape had somehow turned into consensual and enjoyable sex—is able to make sense of it.

None of the published variants offer a viable solution either. Here, the Muzgiz and Nemirovich-Danchenko scores align (more or less): the Nemirovich-Danchenko score reads: "Why did you do that?/I am a married woman" (*Zachem ty sdelal eto? Ya muzhniaia zhena*), while Muzgiz has "Why, why, Seryozha?/I am a married woman." Sergei responds in both sources with "Let's not speak of that," which clearly makes sense. Presumably to smooth the path to Katerina's "I have no husband/only you alone," Sergei's derisive laughter and gloating at R193 is cut completely in both. Katerina enters at R194 with that very line—"I have no husband/only you alone"—and thereafter the three scores are identical, save for both Muzgiz and Nemirovich-Danchenko omitting the final "Darling!" However, even with this more logical flow of dialogue, the postcoital scene remains dramatically flawed: Katerina's question "Why did you do that?" (Nemirovich-Danchenko) or "Why, why Seryozha?" (Muzgiz) hardly sounds like the kind of remark a woman who has just experienced a sexual revelation would make; rather, it sounds like the kind of remark a woman who has been overpowered and raped (but no longer feels threatened) might make. Katerina's miserable protest "I am a married woman" reinforces this negative impression further, even without Sergei's gloating. Her next line, "I have no husband/only you alone" is meant to signal to the audience that she is now in love with Sergei, but unless the staging has already made it clear that the couple are now consensual lovers, the emotional change of gear from her previous line feels impossibly abrupt. That this fundamental dramatic problem was built in from the very start is only highlighted by the alternative text in the draft score: "Don't you dare touch me/I am a married woman." In every single variant from the draft score on, Katerina's opening line is one of rejection, telling Sergei to go, asking him what he did "that" for, or telling him not to touch her.

Although we can surmise that the Nemirovich-Danchenko production used the version of this scene preserved in the printed vocal score, we can be almost certain that Melik-Pashaev conducted this scene in its unexpurgated form for the Bolshoi production of 1935–36. Multiple copies of the 1935 Muzgiz vocal score used in Melik-Pashaev's production are preserved in the Bolshoi archive, and although these show that the whole postcoital dialogue section was deleted (pages crossed out in the scores themselves), this was presumably because Melik-Pashaev was conducting from another score that preserved this scene in its entirety (that is, with the trombone slides and Sergei's "ho ho" intact), rendering the printed Muzgiz scores useless at this point.[16] If Levasheva is correct in her guess that Melik-Pashayev conducted from one of the copyist scores held in the Russian Museum of Musical Culture, then it is indeed certain that the whole postcoital scene was preserved in full at the Bolshoi—perhaps uniquely among the three concurrent productions in 1935. Sadly, Samosud's score (preserved in the Mariinsky Theatre music library) is not accessible to view, so it is not currently possible to reconstruct the Leningrad performance details from his markings.[17] However, the possibility remains that only the Bolshoi production contained the full quota of rehearsal figures in this scene. Thus, the version that Stalin saw was the most sexually exaggerated and crude of all the productions. This detail, combined with what we know of Melik-Pashaev's instructions for the brass to play louder and with raised bells, inevitably raises the question of Stalin's reaction had he gone to the more restrained Nemirovich-Danchenko production.

Clearly, Shostakovich found it difficult to make up his mind about what Katerina was to feel in the crucial moments after sex with Sergei. He wanted to preserve the basic idea from Leskov of Katerina being overpowered by him but immediately falling in love. The idea that Katerina was a virgin was also important at least to Preis, since this detail would render her more innocent according to the presumptions of Soviet courts and public opinion—hence the crude reference to blood on the sheets in the draft libretto and the early draft score.[18] But by raising the level of violence preceding the sex itself, Shostakovich and Preis created a much greater dramatic anomaly than is to be found in Leskov, and this lies principally with the transformation of Sergei's character. In the opera, he initially enters into a dialogue with Katerina that insinuates empathy, but when asked to leave, he quickly becomes a menacing figure, grabbing her, laughing, and saying, "I'm stronger than you" as she cries, "Let go. . . . I'm frightened. . . . I don't wa. . . ." before he overpowers her.

In Leskov, Sergei is less forceful and more persuasive: his declaration of devotion ("I'd gladly take out my steel knife and cut out my poor heart and throw it down by your little feet") may be insincere, but he delivers it, so Leskov tells us, with a tremble in his voice. True, Katerina is suddenly afraid of him, crying out, "Why did you come here? I'll throw myself out of the window" as, Leskov tells us, she is "overwhelmed with ineffable terror." But instead of boasting of his superior strength and laughing at her, Leskov's Sergei simply says, "My matchless sweetheart, why would you want to do that?" as "pulling his young mistress away from the window, he held her tight." Thereupon we see how quickly Leskov's Katerina melts: "'Oh, oh, let go of me', Katerina Lvovna moaned softly, weakening under Sergei's passionate kisses and, in spite of herself, pressing closer still to his powerful body. Sergei lifted his mistress into the air like a child and carried her into a dark corner."[19]

And that is Leskov's sex scene: it delivers the culturally familiar message that Katerina said "no" but meant "yes"; she responded to being overpowered by Sergei not with anguish or fury but with suddenly awakened longing. It is the quintessential rape fantasy of romantic literature, drama, and film only too familiar to us, and evidently to Shostakovich and Preis too. As for the postcoital dialogue, in Leskov it makes perfect sense: "'Go now', said Katerina Lvovna half an hour later. Not looking at Sergei, she was rearranging her dishevelled hair in front of a small mirror. 'Why would I want to do that?' Sergei asked happily. 'My father-in-law will lock the doors'. 'Oh my sweetheart, what kind of men have you known that they can't find their way to a woman except through a door!'" replies Sergei.[20]

In making Sergei so much more violent and unpleasant than he had been in Leskov, Shostakovich and Preis unintentionally set the postcoital dialogue up to fail. Shostakovich wanted Katerina to appear as innocent as possible, and that meant darkening Sergei's character and showing that Katerina was his helpless victim. Leskov's archetypal seduction scene showed Katerina to be more complicit, and there is no suggestion that she might be a virgin. As Yakubov shows, Preis's original libretto had not only invented this detail but also elaborated on it at numerous points, not least at her subsequent murder of her husband Zinovy, where she berates him harshly for "slobbering around unable to do anything." Preis thus made Zinovy's impotence a cause for Katerina's fury for depriving her of sexual fulfillment.[21]

A POSSIBLE SOLUTION?

It may just be possible that the Leningrad Maly production found a way around all of this, and in a manner that points forward to Shostakovich's eventual excision of the sex scene altogether. In Smolich's director's score, held in the Mikhailovsky Theater, the way this scene concludes has again changed. It shows that after the "silent struggle" that concludes with Sergei taking Katerina in his arms, "tightly embracing her," and carrying her behind a curtain, the only dialogue that remains in this scene is prompted by Boris Timofeevich calling to Katerina thus:

B.T.	(behind the door) Katerina!
E.L.	(scared) My father in law!
SER:	holds E.L. in his arms, frozen to the spot
B.T.	(behind the door) Are you in bed?
E.L.	(clutching Sergei in terror) Yes I am
B.T.	(grunts) All right
E.L.	(to Sergei) Now go!
SER.	(stubbornly) I'm not going anywhere
E.L.	(fearfully beseeching Sergei) The old man will lock the doors
SER:	(joyfully) To a fellow like me a window is a door. Come, Katia![22]

In this version, more is left unsaid, and thus left to the audience's imagination. The sex scene itself takes place behind a curtain, so nothing violent (or otherwise) is shown, and—if the draft score changes remained in place—no trombone *glissandi* were left in the score to cheapen the impact of the music. Presumably, Smolich's intention was to cut from R191 to Boris Timofeevich's entry ("Katerina!/Are you in bed?") at R195. This way the action moves straight from an unseen seduction behind a curtain to a visual display of Katerina immediately turning to Sergei for reassurance when she hears Boris Timofeevich at the door at R195; their ensuing dialogue places him in the role of her protector and thus communicates to the audience that they are now lovers, Katerina now ready to trust him completely. Although this solution did not find its way into any version of the score, it does prefigure the later *Katerina Izmailova* scene, where it is the sudden appearance of Boris Timofeevich, together with the alarming timpani figure, that puts a stop to Sergei's violent seduction and instead brings the two together against him, their common enemy.

To summarize, by looking at Leskov's and at Preis's preserved libretto draft, we can see exactly how this sex scene came into being. Preis and Shostakovich, both young men in their twenties at the time of the libretto's creation, accepted the basic trajectory in Leskov of a woman encountering sex for the first time and moving swiftly from being overpowered to being overjoyed. Evidently regarding this as unproblematic, they then used the seduction scene to further underline Sergei's brutal character and Katerina's innocence. But having achieved this end, they were left with the problem of how a woman—even one so deprived of love as Katerina—could really have fallen instantly in love with a man who had taken her with such violence. We have seen the adjustments made to the postcoital dialogue that try to account for it, from having Katerina sound unhappy ("Why, why, Seryozha?") or angry ("Don't you dare touch me") to having her merely urging him to leave ("Now go, for god's sake"), and from having Sergei give the audience graphic details about her virginity, to having him simply gloat over his boss and laugh at her eagerness, to finally having him say hardly anything at all.

It is not surprising that post-1979 productions of the Sikorski version have frequently downplayed the appearance of rape in favor of a consensual scene, showing a rapid switch from violence and resistance to sudden passion.[23] That may be closer to Leskov than to Shostakovich, but it results in a more convincing scene than Preis and Shostakovich had created between them. Those decisions lie wholly in the hands of directors, however, and depend on their perception of Katerina's relative strength and sexual eagerness. It is likely that audiences today would be less tolerant of a display of sexual violence if it were followed by adoring submission, and staging it that way would foreground a major weakness in the opera's scenario that can instead be effectively circumvented by thoughtful direction. Nevertheless, it is curious to see how even in the early 1930s, Smolich was also apparently uncomfortable about this interpretation. His solution—to conceal the sexual encounter completely and remove all the problematic dialogue—was an effective way of turning a threatened rape into something that could at least be imagined to be more consensual. From all the sources dating from the 1930s that I have been able to view, Smolich's staging is the only one that offers us a textual route to resolving this dilemma.

KATERINA IZMAILOVA

Shostakovich may have thought back to Smolich's radical solution when revising *Lady Macbeth* as *Katerina Izmailova*. Perhaps with the passing of time, and his own age and life experience having matured his perspective on such matters, Shostakovich came to feel that the best solution was to cut even more radically. Smolich had at least retained nearly all the original music, in all its terrifying power. But Shostakovich went much further when preparing *Katerina Izmailova*. Here, there is no sexual encounter at all, because at the very point where Sergei launches his attack on Katerina, precipitating her struggle, Shostakovich cut off any further development by the stage directions he indicated in the score: Boris Timofeevich appears at the window, terrifying both of them. His sudden appearance is signaled by a *fortissimo* triplet motif (percussion, then full orchestra) that continues for fourteen bars; then we return to the original dialogue, now tidied up once and for all by Shostakovich: Katerina: "Now go, for god's sake/I am a married woman" (*Uidi ty, radi boga/Ved' ia muzh-niaia zhena*); Sergei: "You don't love your husband" (*Ty muzha ne liubish'*); Katerina: "I made a vow to my husband/Don't ruin me" (*Kliatvu dala muzhu/Ne gubi menia*); Boris Timofeevich interpolates; thereafter all sources are more or less identical, with only the substitution of "Come, Katia!" with "My Katia!"

This creates an entirely different impression, just as Shostakovich intended it to. Sergei does not assault Katerina, though the scene up to Boris Timofeevich's appearance has been the same as in *Lady Macbeth*, with the same physical struggle as Sergei begins to overpower Katerina (this can also be seen clearly in the film version). Once Boris has interrupted them, Sergei is no longer a physical threat to Katerina: true, she asks him to go and he doesn't; but he also alludes to her loveless state, and when she finally goes to him, she does so willingly. We do not see what passes between them, but Shostakovich has prepared the dialogue carefully to show that they will go on to become lovers consensually. He has removed the offensive implication that a woman can be simultaneously raped and seduced. In doing so, he drew closer to Leskov, and, though Katerina is less of a victim as a result (and Sergei less violent), the scene makes perfect dramatic sense.

CHAPTER 4

SEX, SOCIETY, AND SOVIET FEMININITY

I F WE CAN BEGIN to understand why aspects of the libretto in the Act One sex scene feel disjunctive, other questions remain. We might wonder, for instance, why a young Soviet composer seeking to make his mark in a high-stakes cultural environment felt that not one, but two scenes of sexual assault in a new opera would not only be acceptable to Soviet audiences (including the ever-important "mass listener") but also acceptable to the censorship bodies, any officials who would be likely to see the opera, and music critics and peers. This alone is a tangled question, with many possible answers and caveats, and it needs to be addressed carefully.

In the first place, Shostakovich chose *Lady Macbeth* as his source text during the late 1920s: in an article published

Shostakovich's Lady Macbeth of the Mtsensk District. Pauline Fairclough, Oxford University Press.
© Oxford University Press 2025. DOI: 10.1093/9780197534977.003.0004

in *Sovetskoe iskusstvo* in 1932, he informed the reader that he had by then worked on the opera for about two and half years, which would take his start date to some point in 1929.[1] These years—1929 to April 1932—were some of the least congenial for creative artists in the early Soviet period. Although *Lady Macbeth* received its premiere right in the middle of the brief period of liberalization that came after the April 1932 resolution that closed down all cultural factions and replaced them with single unions, it was conceived and composed at the peak of proletarian authority in the arts. Indeed, the resolution itself was something no one could have predicted, coming very abruptly at a moment when the proletarians' power seemed, if anything, to be gaining the upper hand permanently.[2] What this means is that, at the time when Shostakovich first began work on *Lady Macbeth*, the cultural environment was extremely challenging, with any new opera likely to be pored over by hostile proletarian militants—the same militants who had brought the run of his first opera *The Nose* to a premature end in 1930. But another change in Soviet society had come already in 1928. Stalin ended Lenin's experiment in kick-starting the Soviet economy, the New Economic Policy (NEP) era, in favor of Five-Year Plans. The NEP was still in the process of being discredited and blamed for a range of social ills including profiteering, antisocial behavior, and general decadence (all associated with the West), and this has relevance for *Lady Macbeth*, as will be seen.

In this chapter we will consider the scene of sexual violence that Shostakovich did *not* cut in the 1950s: the assault upon the housekeeper Aksinia by Sergei and male workers in the Izmailov household. In modern-day productions, this scene is invariably where the real violence and sexual "shock factor" lie. Although the score indicates sexual molestation with Aksinia groped as she is rolled around in a barrel, directors since the 1980s have tended to stage it more directly as a rape, as I will discuss below. But was it really acceptable to place something so sexually explicit and violent on the Soviet stage in the 1930s? To answer this question, we will look at both social and dramatic contexts for this scene but also question whether the sexual violence we now see onstage in modern productions is a reasonable interpretation of the way it was originally conceived.

WOMEN IN THE NEW SOVIET SOCIETY

Russia was hardly unique in having a major problem with endemic sexual violence. But after the Bolshevik Revolution, it was unique in having a government that might have been expected to embed sexual equality into policy and thus develop a particularly robust approach to tackling rape, domestic abuse, and other forms of violent social behaviors against women. And in certain respects, particularly regarding women's right to a full education and skilled professional work, the Soviet Union was ahead of much more ostensibly advanced industrialized nations. Soviet women were training in large numbers as engineers, doctors, and scientists already in the 1920s: Shostakovich's first wife Nina was herself a physicist. The Bolsheviks had established the *Zhenotdel* (Women's section) in 1919, a department specifically addressing women's interests. Early feminist Bolsheviks like Alexandra Kollontai and Inessa Armand were tasked with developing socioeconomic strategies to improve the rights and lot of Soviet women, initially at least with Lenin's apparent blessing. Lenin envisaged a future in which Bolshevik society would release women from, as the historian Pavla Vesela has argued, quoting Lenin directly, "their stultifying and humiliating resignation to the perpetual and exclusive atmosphere of the kitchen and nursery."[3] And one of the earliest new Bolshevik laws dispensed with the old bureaucracy for securing divorce: Vesela again quotes Lenin directly, this time from a speech delivered on November 19, 1918, at the All-Russian Congress of Women Workers: "the Soviet government has completely abolished the source of bourgeois filth, repression and humiliation— divorce proceedings."[4]

But, as Barbara Evans Clements, Thomas G. Schrand, and others have argued, the male Bolshevik leadership was half-hearted about the wider "feminist" project, and by the late 1920s, the decision to pursue "socialism in one country" led to prioritizing industrialization and the expansion of heavy industry at the expense of "softer" projects like housing, consumer industry, childcare, and other social services recommended by the *Zhenotdel*.[5] The *Zhenotdel* was closed down in 1930 and its challenge to the nuclear family was renounced. Its remaining policy—the placing of women on par with men in the paid Soviet labor force—was retained, but not at the expense of freeing women from traditional domestic roles. As Schrand shows, the "Five-Year Plan for Labour" drawn up in 1930 advocated exploiting female labor from male worker households on the grounds that factories could expand their workforce without expanding worker housing. But the plan made it clear that women were still expected to shoulder the full range of domestic duties.

One of the unintended effects of this push to include women in the labor market was a drastic fall in birth rate: as Schrand observes, "In 1928 [the year the industrialization and collectivization programs began], there were 43.7 births per thousand people and 130 abortions per thousand births. In following years, the annual number of births steadily fell and the number of abortions soared; by 1934, the birthrate dropped to 30.1, while the abortion rate reached 271."[6] This population decline had obvious implications for the future Soviet workforce. Together with steps to address personal responsibility for cleaner living conditions and food hygiene, the threat to productivity would swiftly be addressed in new policies. Early Bolshevik support for women's rights as Soviet citizens was tempered by fear that these liberated women posed an existential risk to social survival. As Clements has argued, "The Bolsheviks perceived the sexual experimentation and marital instability of the twenties as a threat because they feared, rather than hoped for, the dissolution of the family."[7]

Economics and deep-rooted social patriarchalism, then, proved strong motivations for changing Soviet social policy to an aggressive pronatalism, and abortion would become illegal under new laws in 1936. But sexual violence against women was also addressed in Bolshevik laws: the prison sentence for rape in 1926 was a maximum of five years, eight years if the victim had been gang-raped, was underage, or had committed suicide as a result. In legal practice (though not in law itself), however, the victim's virginity was commonly cited as an aggravating factor when determining sentencing and even the guilt of the accused, as Dan Healey has shown.[8]

Believing that virginity was something that could be physically proven by examination, doctors certified women and girls as either sexually active or virgins once a rape allegation had been made. Their conclusions could result in the victim losing her case and—just as seriously—losing her reputation within her social community. Even relatively enlightened laws could not overturn long-standing social conditioning and outdated medical practice. The emphasis laid on virginity at the point of rape in court judgments was presumably why Preis took such care to present Katerina as a virgin in his draft libretto: it was a way of underlining her innocence at the same time as making Sergei even more of a predator.

There was, however, a Leningrad rape case that received both unprecedented media attention and unusually severe punishment in the years immediately preceding work on *Lady Macbeth*, and that was the Chubarov Alley gang rape of September 1926. A young woman was set upon by a group of young men returning home from a funeral and gang-raped over a period of two hours in Leningrad. Incredibly, the woman survived and was able to report the crime. The men were arrested and put on trial in December 1926: twenty-two out of twenty-six accused were found guilty not just of rape, but of the more severe charge of "banditry." This elevation of guilt from rape (maximum sentence eight years) to banditry enabled the judge to pass unusually severe sentences. Seven of the men were sentenced to death, three received ten-year prison terms, and three received eight-year sentences (the others received lighter sentences). Eric Naiman, whose study of this episode is still the best available source in English, notes that the outraged response in the Leningrad and national press reflected a number of sociopolitical anxieties linked with this specific case. First, the victim was a peasant who had moved to the city to study at a Rabfak—a form of higher educational institution for workers—making her an ideal example of new Soviet womanhood. Second, the perpetrators were themselves factory workers, and five of them were members of the Komsomol, the official Communist youth organization. Third, the attack coincided with a press campaign against "hooliganism" that was linked with the legacy of war communism and Lenin's flagship policy, the NEP. The papers showed a marked inclination to identify a deeper social cause for the crime; Naiman quotes a Soviet journalist who led a campaign against the poet Sergei Esenin:

> The least resistant of our young people are poorly withstanding the test of NEP, of this ordeal that is far more difficult than the fire of war. Deprivation, inequality, our disorganized way of life, the influence of bourgeois and semibourgeois elements—all these often sully and crush the young, untempered soul.[9]

Naiman shows that horror at the attack itself was not sufficient cause for the prominence this case received in the Soviet press. Gang rapes were not especially unusual in Soviet society; Naiman refers to a 1927 collection of rural crimes to show that they were usually perpetrated on festive occasions after drinking, and Healey presents the case of a peasant woman gang-raped on International Women's Day, 1928—just over a year after these stiff sentences were passed in Leningrad.[10] It was the fact that both the victim and perpetrators were members of the officially elevated social groups of workers, peasants and Komsomol members, that deeper causes for the crimes were sought and found both in the press and in court. The Soviet press was, in effect, reporting on one of their own: not bourgeois "degenerates" but young Soviet workers, Komsomol members, men who should have been the pride of Soviet youth. In passing sentence, the judge and media alike practiced a form of ideological cleansing, which both identified the cause of the social problems responsible (the NEP and the legacy of war communism) and proposed the solution: death or imprisonment to the offenders.

Shostakovich and Preis, like all other Leningraders who read the newspapers, knew about the Chubarov Alley case. But though it was a real-life event, anxiety about sexual behavior swiftly found its way into Soviet literature and theater, and this melding of real crime with fiction and drama underlines the prominence of sexual violence in the late 1920s. Naiman comments on three stories featuring sexual attacks on women published in 1926 and 1927 that attracted especially harsh press attention: Panteleimon Romanov's "Without Cherry Blossoms," Sergei Malashkin's "The Moon from the Right Side," and Lev Gumilevsky's *Dog Alley*. In depicting these depraved acts by young Soviet men, the authors were accused in the Komsomol and workers' press of slandering Soviet youth. In his defense, Gumilevsky declared, "I had followed Lenin's dictates [regarding proper sexual relations between men and women]. . . . 'We must fearlessly admit the existence of evil so that we can struggle against it decisively.'"[11] In raising the topic of sexual abuse in fiction, each of these writers sought to support what they perceived to be government interests in stamping out such behavior, as Naiman concludes. None intended to court controversy. Indeed, in the wake of the Chubarov Alley reportage, a writer accused of indecency or slander for describing sexual assault might justifiably have referred critics directly to this case.

It was not only in these three fictional works that the theme of sexual assault was explored in Soviet artworks. Sergei Tretiakov's play *I Want a Baby!*, written in 1926 but banned before Meyerhold could stage it in his 1927–28 season, featured a gang rape near a factory—just as the Chubarov Alley attack had been. And Jennifer Wilson has convincingly shown that the play Meyerhold chose as a substitute for *I Want a Baby!*—Alexander Griboedov's well-known drama *Woe from Wit* (*Gore ot uma*, 1823)— contained crucially similar themes of sexual violence, at least in Meyerhold's particular staging of it under the title *Woe to Wit*.[12] Alma Hanson Law's reconstruction of staging based on detailed production notes shows that the scene in which the elderly character Pavel Famusov harasses the maid Liza attracted special attention from Meyerhold: "[The scene] is very true, subtle, and not what a podborodoček feels. That's rubbish. This is a physical scene, a difficult scene. (17/XII/27)." Law clarifies the meaning of Meyerhold's note on "podborodoček": "From the Russian, 'little chin.' Meyerhold uses the term to mean 'an old fellow who goes around tickling the maid under the chin,' in other words, someone who is always after the maid."[13] Law also shows that Meyerhold wanted to make Famusov into an especially unpleasant character, far from the older stage portrayals Soviet audiences were used to:

Traditionally, Meyerhold said, Famusov is played as a "cheerful eccentric," a flabby old fellow who "playfully tickles the maid under the chin." . . . In contrast, Meyerhold saw Famusov as a man of fifty, or even forty, energetic and malicious, a thievish beast of prey.[14]

In Griboedov, Famusov is harmless. In Meyerhold, as Law has shown us, he grabs hold of Liza and spanks her as she struggles to escape from him.[15] Moreover, Meyerhold instructed the actor playing this role to laugh continually while carrying out the assault: "your laughter has to be stronger than these words so that the words are just barely heard—a long unbroken, almost legato laughter with a huge reserve. The laughter is endless . . . so that there's not so much Liza in this scene as laughter."[16] Using fake humor to underline the violence of Famusov's assault was a stroke of genius. As we will see, this interpretive decision may well have influenced Shostakovich's and Smolich's staging of the assault of the housekeeper Aksinia in Act One of *Lady Macbeth*. The revised character of Famusov himself is also an obvious prototype for Boris Timofeevich, similarly rendered younger than his original literary age, and transformed into a sexual predator as well as a bully (figure 4.1).

Finally, as we consider the changing image of Soviet womanhood through the 1920s and into the 1930s, Fyodor Gladkov's novel *Cement* (*Tsement*, 1925) provides an ideal case study for showing both contemporary attitudes to rape and changing depictions of male-female relationships and women specifically. Gladkov revised the novel repeatedly, gradually constraining the originally feminist

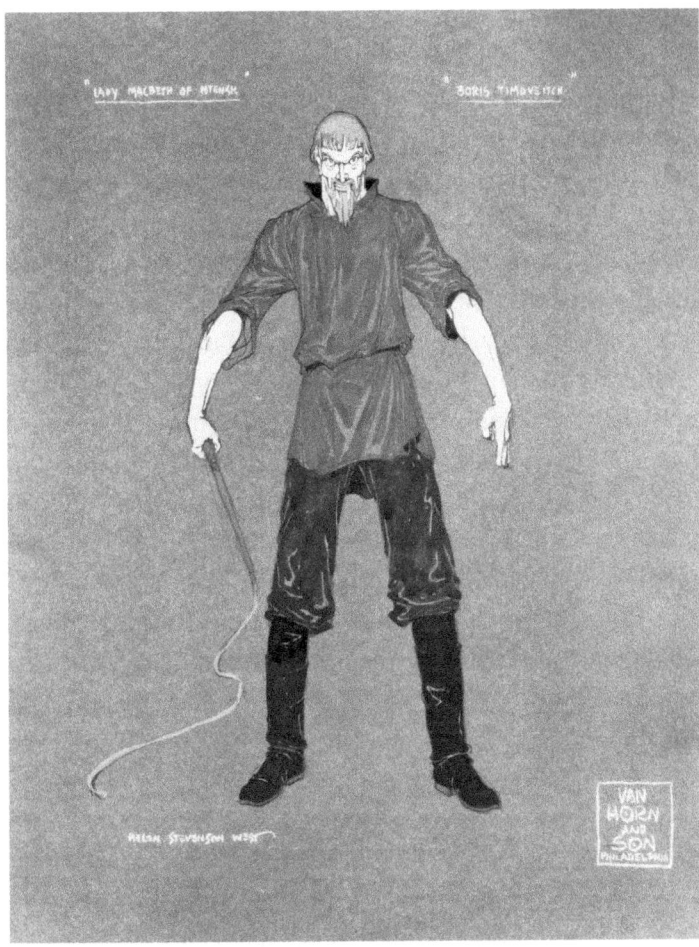

FIG. 4.1 Boris Timofeevich, costume design for Cleveland production, 1935. Illustration by Van Horn and Sons, copy courtesy of The Cleveland Orchestra Archives.

portrayal of the main female character Dasha and subjecting it to an increasingly marked male gaze, as Pavla Vesela has shown.[17] Gladkov also revised accounts of both rape and consensual sex in the original (written between 1922 and 1924) to be less shocking and to delegitimize a woman's sex drive in favor of her desire for motherhood.

In the original version of the novel, Gleb, a returned Civil War soldier, expects his wife Dasha to play the traditional roles in his household. But Dasha is already a "New Soviet Woman" who wears male clothing, has her hair cut short, and has put their child into a communal children's home. Initially shocked, Gleb gradually evolves into a New Soviet Man, who accepts these role changes. But in the Stalinist version written in 1939–40, Dasha is considerably more submissive and feminized; her various affairs with other male characters are erased while her near abandonment of their child in the home (who eventually dies) is softened as the reader is shown how happy the child is there. Upon learning of her death, the original Dasha remained stoic, but with tears in her eyes. In the Stalinist version, she weeps helplessly while Gleb watches her. Gladkov also transforms Dasha's attitude toward her husband in later versions: no longer does she teach him how to improve himself and turn away from his old patriarchal ideas, now she is more submissive, more maternal, no longer sexually assertive and thus threatening his male dominance.

In his own discussion of the original version of *Cement*, Naiman shows how the local Bolshevik chair of the executive committee, Badin, seduces Dasha: "his blood was streaming into her body through his arms, lips and nostrils, and in answer to these strong pulsations a wave of feminine weakness passed languorously through her veins, a wave of confused pleasure and fear."[18] Dasha, herself a strong female character, is well matched to Badin, even though he is not her husband. At various points in the novel, she is shown to rely on his physical strength and to appreciate it. But when Badin forces himself on the weaker female character Polia, Gladkov makes a clear distinction between the experiences of the two women: Polia is helpless and afraid, physically too weak to resist him, and traumatized by her experience. While Dasha is seduced, Polia is raped—and both by the same man.[19] Rape is not sanctioned in *Cement* by any means: in wanting to celebrate the Bolshevik Badin's masculine power, Gladkov allowed him a scene of convincing seduction; but in showing that he has a darker side, he demonstrated that this strong male character could also force himself on women, damaging them both physically and psychologically.

AKSINIA'S ASSAULT

We now return to the point at which Shostakovich and Preis were drafting their libretto, just a few years after the Chubarov Alley case and the animated cultural response to it. Both certainly knew Gladkov's *Cement*, as it was a key literary text of the period. And they, like Gladkov, clearly believed that their heroine could melt in the strong arms of a powerful male—albeit protesting and struggling far more than Dasha did in *Cement*. But what about the other female character assaulted by Sergei in Act One: not the heroine, but a bona fide member of the working class?

Act One Scene Four shows the housekeeper Aksinia under attack from male workers. The stage directions printed in all the scores tell us exactly what is going on: "They [workers] have put Aksinia in a barrel open at both ends and won't let her out." However, Smolich's staging of this scene as preserved in the director's score held at the Mikhailovsky Theater reveals not only further specifics of staging but also tone of voice—how the men speak to Aksinia as she is attacked and how she responds—and, critically, the way Katerina enters the scene, bringing Aksinia's assault to an abrupt end. Some of the libretto quoted below is preserved in the printed scores, but there are words and phrases in Smolich's score that did not appear in the Nemirovich-Danchenko or Muzgiz scores and are not even found in the "unexpurgated" Sikorski score. In all 1930s sources, the language used by characters in this scene is highly colloquial and vulgar. In those numerous instances where literal rendering in English makes no sense, I have used what seem to me to be the nearest modern-day English-equivalent expressions. I quote here from Smolich's director's score; where quoting and translating directly, material is placed in quotation marks; elsewhere I summarize.

Even before the start of the scene at R70, Smolich's directions indicate that Aksinia is seized and placed in the barrel at R68: "Sergei seizes Aksinia by the waist with both hands and drags her into the yard to the barn. At this moment, an empty barrel is rolled out of the barn. Sergei and workers throw Aksinia into the barrel. General hilarity." Opening with Aksinia's terrified keening "Ay!," the music in this scene is fast and aggressive, the men's chorus throughout insulting Aksinia in driven, (almost) uniform quarter-note textures. Both Sergei's and Aksinia's lines are high-pitched, denoting frenzied attack and panic, respectively. Toward the end of the assault, the tempo quickens from *Allegro* to *Presto* (from half-note 112 to 132) and Sergei's cries become more like gasps; in the final section the male chorus's rising pitches signify that Sergei's assault is reaching its climax, with his final triumphant cries of "Hey!" dominating Aksinia's distressed "Pusti!" (let go!).

Though the music is terrifying in its driven violence, the stage directions are ambiguous when it comes to determining the nature of Sergei's attack. Aksinia is rolled around the stage in an open-ended barrel while Sergei molests her viciously, but it is not clear whether Shostakovich and Smolich staged his assault as a rape. Even at the end of the stage directions, we see that the rolling doesn't stop, and at the climax of the scene (from R85), the men have recommenced rolling her, and it seems probable that Sergei's "Hey!" relates to this, rather than to her rape (as is commonly staged in modern productions).[20] As we see from Smolich's staging detailed below, at the point where most modern directors have Sergei simulating rape of Aksinia (from R87), in Leningrad he is rolling her in the barrel along with all the other men (figure 4.2):

R70 (start of Scene Four proper): Aksinia: "Oh, you shameless one, don't pinch me. Ow, it hurts/What are you doing? Shameless devil, what are you doing?"[21]

Male workers cluster around Aksinia, mocking her voice ("a pig is singing like a nightingale"), her nose ("big enough for seven"), and her plumpness ("You could make cutlets from her leg"). Sergei pushes Aksinia back into the barrel, not letting her out; Aksinia: "lousy devil, get off me!"[22] At R74, Sergei gets into the barrel with Aksinia; she tries to get away, swearing, "Svoloch!" (you bastard!) and tearing at his hair. At R75, Aksinia "cries out in pain." To general laughter, Sergei turns to the workers with outstretched hand, shouting, "Milk!" At R76 Aksinia hits his hand and

FIG. 4.2 *Lady Macbeth*, Act One, Scene Two: Aksinia being rolled in the barrel. Cleveland production, 1935. Photo by Geoffrey Landesman, courtesy of The Cleveland Orchestra Archives.

kicks him: "You bastard, I'm all bruised." Workers (jeering): "So?" Sergei: Milk on my hand! By God, milk! Worker ("examining Sergei's hand with curiosity"): "Let me see!" Sergei ("pushes her again into the barrel maliciously"): "But she has a pimply face." Aksinia ("hides again in the barrel and is afraid to get out"), at R77: "You shameless one, my breasts are all bruised, my skirt is torn" (laughter). Sergei "coaxes Aksinia out of the barrel" and laughs at her. At R78 Aksinia tries to escape from Sergei, but he forcefully pushes her back into the barrel and tells the workers to start rolling it. They roll the barrel back and forth. At R79 the tempo quickens to *Presto* (half-note = 132) and Aksinia cries for help; at R80 Sergei instructs them to stop rolling the barrel; Aksinia climbs out and attacks Sergei. At R81 Sergei overpowers her and forces her back into the barrel;

he then orders the men to roll the barrel even harder. At R82 Aksinia, "crying pitifully," shouts again for help and Sergei responds, "Keep still you bitch" (*stoi suka*). Aksinia evidently doesn't stop struggling, as at R83 everyone is still trying to force her to stay in the barrel and at R84 Sergei is also directed to push her in again. At this point, poor Aksinia, "worn out," can only gasp "Oh" (*Ay!*), but at R85 the men again commence barrel rolling; "choking with laughter," they sing, "he'll make us die laughing."

At this point, Smolich's directions show that Katerina, overhearing the uproar, gets up from the divan in the dining room, puts on her scarf, and goes quickly into the yard. She thus witnesses Aksinia crying again "You bastard!" and sees Sergei swinging his arms to indicate that the barrel should be rolled even faster; at R87 the directions indicate Sergei "rolling barrel, joining in the excitement" (*vkhodit v azart*) and Aksinia continuing to try and escape ("Let go, you dog" [*kobel*]). Now, at R88, Katerina appears on the forestage: "While they are laughing, Katerina Lvovna appears on the porch. Seeing Aksinia, dishevelled and upset, inside the barrel, she laughingly looks on at the struggle. She holds a handful of sunflower seeds."

Textual changes from the libretto as presented in the staging score and those to be found in printed sources from the 1930s, though minor, were focused on making the language marginally less vulgar at certain points, and even the Sikorski score does not include Sergei's "Keep still you bitch," having instead "Keep still, woman!" (*Stoi, baba!*) or his cries of "Milk! Milk!" (*Moloko!*), replacing it with "Khorosho!"— meaning simply "great!" "Keep still you bitch," however, is preserved in the Nemirovich-Danchenko score, but the printed libretto for that production replaces "bitch" with "woman." This score also preserves the text where Sergei sings "Moloko!"—although again the Nemirovich-Danchenko libretto has a slight variant: "Moloko!" becomes "Khorosho." This suggests that the change was made not to avoid offense but because Shostakovich was persuaded that "Khorosho" was just a better word to use at that point. This variant is also to be found in the 1935 Muzgiz score and in the Sikorski score.

Having established precisely what took place on the Leningrad stage in 1934 and precisely what was sung both there and in Moscow, we are in a position to ponder exactly what this scene is aiming to depict. Writing in the late 1940s, the musicologist Rena Moisenko openly called the scene a rape: "the shrieks of pain of the raped girl intermingle with coarse and cynical comments from the crowd of onlookers."[23] Frustratingly, given that the annotated libretto draft that Manashir Yakubov used when preparing the New Collected Works edition of *Lady Macbeth* seems to be currently missing from the Shostakovich Archive, and Yakubov did not address this scene in his short essay for that volume, we cannot determine how Preis originally conceived of it, let alone what Shostakovich opted to keep and what to omit or change. But although I found not a single contemporary press review that alluded to Aksinia being raped, there was one writer who did regard it as such, and he did so in his own essay for the Maly program booklet: the eminent Soviet musicologist and composer Boris Asafiev. He writes of Aksinia, "There is a woman, insulted for her physical appearance, and who is raped."[24]

Did the opera's original audiences perceive the barrel rolling as a metaphor for actual rape? Was the constant laughter accompanying the barrel rolling intended to signal that the scene was comedic, or did it echo that grotesque moment in Meyerhold's *Woe to Wit*, where Famusov laughs long and loud as he assaults Liza? Did Shostakovich deliberately juxtapose an attack of brutal sexual violence (with music to match) with staged hilarity, all the better to make his critical point about the degraded lives of workers in Nicholas I's Russia? This last is a real possibility. Having Aksinia getting in and out of the barrel and being rolled around onstage was an effective way of staging the attack: if all the focus is on Sergei raping Aksinia, then the crowd of men onstage have little to do and the scene can even become somewhat static.[25] If the men are instead directed to participate in the action, grabbing at Aksinia, tearing off her clothes, and so forth (as in Martin Kušej's 2006 Dutch National Opera production), then the whole scene becomes something between a rape (Sergei penetrating Aksinia) and a gang rape, with all the men onstage participating in the assault, even if only one fully rapes her.[26]

Notwithstanding heightened public awareness of sexual violence and even its appearance in contemporary drama and fiction in late 1920s Leningrad, Shostakovich and Smolich could hardly stage nudity and rape to the degree that has become common in late twentieth-century and twenty-first-century opera houses. It would be reasonable to regard the barrel rolling as a powerful metaphor for Aksinia's rape; at the very least, she is sexually molested inside the barrel.

But the scene becomes more complex: as far as the printed scores are concerned, Katerina enters; the attack abruptly ends; and, after a final skirmish between Aksinia and Sergei, Katerina delivers her lecture to Sergei on his attitude to women ("Leave the woman alone; you enjoy making fun of a woman"). Smolich's score, however, paints a very different picture of the Leningrad staging; I will quote directly in translation from it here:

KATERINA: stands on the porch, looking at Aksinia; laughingly asks her, "What's up with you?"

AKSINIA: (fixes skirt) "My skirt is all torn."

KATERINA: (stifling her laughter, eating sunflower seeds) "Let the woman go; you enjoy making fun of a woman."

SERGEI (swaggers forward): "Well, what else is there to make fun of?"

KATERINA (standing on the porch, still stifling her laughter): "And is that all a woman is for?"

SERGEI (looking at Katerina impudently and slyly): "What else are they there for?"

Following Aksinia's furious irruption into this dialogue and her subsequent departure from the scene, Katerina rather languidly begins to further berate Sergei, only gradually becoming serious:

Katerina (stands on the porch, folds her hands, and looks ironically at Sergei with a smile): "You men think too much of yourselves. You think you are strong, that only you are brave, only you are clever. (seriously, firmly): but don't you know of the women who feed their families, and even fight on the battlefield, killing the enemy?"

As Sergei turns away, shrugging his shoulders, the stage directions are unusually explicit: "there is a pause, and then suddenly a change in her voice becomes apparent, she gazes into the distance and her voice grows tender and serious." She adds, "Many sacrificed themselves for their husbands and dear ones." Sergei, alerted by the new warmth in Katerina's tone, turns back and approaches her; but as she concludes her speech, she flirtatiously (*igrivo*) throws her remaining sunflower seeds into his face, causing him to jump away and rub his eyes.

These stage directions, long since forgotten, bear no resemblance to the tone of this scene in modern productions and quite possibly differ from the way the scene was played out in the Nemirovich-Danchenko theater as well. Katerina's text—taken at face value—is serious, and her music is certainly not playful in tone. In one of the darkest keys, that of E-flat minor, cast in a slow march, Katerina's lines are steady, somber, slowing the dramatic pace and regulating the tone after the helter-skelter of the previous section. And it is precisely because of this tone that directors interpret this moment as a serious speech. Without these directions, her image as a late and largely passive participant in the men's laughter at Aksinia's expense and her flirtatious smiling at Sergei, then throwing seeds in his face, are erased from the scene, and we are left with only a solemn lecture. In the absence of Preis's draft, but mindful of what he did with the subsequent sex scene between Sergei and Katerina, referring to Leskov might prove helpful here.

In the novella, the scene is presented as an amusing skirmish, the result of high spirits on a beautiful sunny day:

"What's making you all so happy?" Katerina Lvovna asked her father-in-law's stewards. "We've been weighing a live sow, Katerina Lvovna" one of them replied. "What sow?" "A sow called Aksinia, ma'am . . . " said a young man with a bold, cheerful face. . . . Just then, out of the pan hanging from the crossbeams of the weighing scales, appeared the plump rosy face of Aksinia the cook. "You devils, you slippery devils!" she cursed, trying to seize hold of the iron beam and climb out of the swaying pan. "She weighs twenty stone before dinner and if she eats another basket of hay there won't be weights enough to weigh her with" said the handsome young man. Turning the pan over, he tipped the cook out onto a pile of sacks in the corner. Cursing merrily, the woman began to tidy herself up. "All right—and how much do *I* weigh?" said Katerina Lvovna. Grabbing hold of the ropes, she jumped up onto the pan. "Nine and a half stone," said handsome young Sergei, after throwing some weights into the other pan. "A marvel!" "What's to marvel at?" "That you weigh even nine and a half stone, Katerina Lvovna. The way I see it, a woman like you should be carried about in a man's arms the whole livelong day."[27]

After a little more charming back-and-forth, where Katerina blushes at Sergei's compliments and "feels a sudden longing to let her hair down," the pair of them wrestle, as in the opera. And it is after this scene (no Boris Timofeevich appearing to spoil their fun) that Aksinia tells Katerina that she should be careful of Sergei and that she believes he carried on with his previous mistress, resulting in his being fired. In the opera, it is Aksinia's warning, delivered *before* she is attacked, that is implied by the staging to be the cause of Sergei's vengeful assault, as Smolich directed Sergei to lurk in the background to overhear Aksinia's gossip to Katerina. Shostakovich and Preis opted to retain the warning, but because their more violent scene had resulted in Aksinia's departure from the stage, and Aksinia herself was reduced to a furious, distressed condition, they moved it to an earlier point, just after Katerina has been forced to swear fidelity to her husband before he departs on business. Sergei's overhearing her words is thereby understood to be the motivation for his attack on her in the very next moments, thereby making her at least to some degree the agent of her misfortune.

If Shostakovich and Preis can be suspected of diluting audience sympathy for Aksinia by showing her gossip to be the cause of Sergei's assault, they went much further than even Leskov in depicting her as unattractive—presumably to contrast with the beautiful Katerina. Aksinia is described unkindly in Smolich's score as a "freckled, fat, snub-nosed peasant woman"—a perfect fit for comic-book masculine teasing in a way that a more vulnerable-looking young girl would not have been (figure 4.3). Shostakovich and Preis could have transformed Aksinia into a figure more guaranteed to evince audience sympathy, but they kept her physical appearance at a distance from Katerina's, doubtless in part to enable the men's unpleasant comments on her looks, but also surely to lessen the extent of the audience's sympathy for her.

Preis and Shostakovich transformed a comic scene of teasing Aksinia for her weight into one of sexual violence, whether we understand it as a rape or not. Katerina's late entry, and her good-humored participation, was

FIG. 4.3 Costume design for Aksinia. Cleveland production, 1935. Illustration by Van Horn and Sons, copy courtesy of The Cleveland Orchestra Archives.

preserved: she was never intended to march in and launch into a feminist harangue, thereby alienating a large section of the contemporary Soviet audience. Rather, she is initially complicit, and it is only when faced with Sergei's indifference that she attracts his attention by introducing a gentler note into her speech; having succeeded in capturing his interest, she flirts further by throwing seeds into his face. For all the moral weight placed on this scene in modern productions of *Lady Macbeth*, it was manifestly not how Smolich, for one, envisaged Katerina's participation.

Although I don't believe we can be certain that Shostakovich conceived of Aksinia's assault as a rape scene, there are conclusions that we can draw about how the Leningrad production, at least, approached it. First, Aksinia is introduced as an unattractive gossip, whose words are overheard. She is subjected to extremely unpleasant abuse and sexual assault, principally from Sergei, but when it is over, Katerina—who has witnessed the last stages of the assault—laughs at her along with the men. In the opera as in Leskov, the scene functions dramatically as a signal to the spectator (or reader) that Katerina is attracted to Sergei, but also that he is dangerous. Indeed if, as Asafiev believed, Sergei (metaphorically) rapes Aksinia, then we could conclude that Shostakovich wished us to understand that Sergei's superficial charm has a dark side: he is powerful, coercive, and a dangerous bully. Katerina's laughter at the close of the attack, however, would seem to negate Asafiev's interpretation: how can we sympathize with a heroine who finds another woman's rape amusing? The obvious answer is that Aksinia was not raped and that what Katerina saw was the final barrel rolling, which appeared to her perhaps unkind but harmless and, at least initially, funny.[28]

My personal view is that Shostakovich and Preis did not intend the audience to feel too sorry for Aksinia, reserving their compassion for Katerina alone. At the same time, they wanted to darken Leskov's scene and show the audience the "real" Sergei before they see him in Katerina's bedroom. But again, the transfer of events and characters from the novella to the libretto was not entirely successful, and this can be seen in Katerina's flippant response to Aksinia's plight. If she witnessed Aksinia's full-scale rape, then her flirtation with Sergei (their wrestling match) strikes an odd note, and her subsequent passion for him seems even less creditable. The only reading that leaves Katerina's own character intact is the lighter one: that Aksinia's assault was not rape, violently sexual though it certainly was; that Katerina witnesses only (literally, not metaphorically) her being rolled in a barrel and fails to realize the seriousness of Aksinia's distress; and finally, that Katerina, ignorant of how the scene has played out from the start, begins to fall into Sergei's clutches even as she berates him for teasing women. In short, the scene sets a trap for Katerina in both novella and opera, awakening both her interest in Sergei and Sergei's own awareness that Katerina might be a suitable target for his next erotic escapade.

CHANGING POLITICS OF RECEPTION

In light of these details, we can return to the question of why Shostakovich believed that staging sexual violence would be found acceptable, especially given the difficult cultural period of *Lady Macbeth*'s composition. Answers can be found in the shift in the way women were treated as workers both in the public space and in the home during the post-NEP era, which impacted how women, and sexual behaviors in general, were reflected in art, literature, and drama. But the peculiar circumstances of *Lady Macbeth*'s chronology mean that the opera was conceived in one era but received its final, fatal critique in another. Shostakovich planned it during a time when the arts were still absorbing the shocking Chubarov Alley case and the media was focused on male sexual violence as a current social problem. It was not controversial to address these issues in art: it was even fashionable, so long as the targets were not young Soviet youth. By making the perpetrator a social degenerate of Tsarist society, Shostakovich was in safe territory. Meyerhold's *Woe to Wit*, showing mild sexual violence, was staged in the 1927–28 season and was one of his longest-running and most successful productions. Similarly, Gladkov's *Cement* (featuring several descriptions of sex and rape) was widely praised and accepted as a classic of new Soviet literature. We must also remember that the scene with Aksinia could easily be perceived as nothing more than molestation and teasing, however unpleasant; the constant laughter and hilarity present in the scene even admit the possibility that it could be taken as comedic play. Given that not a single contemporary review (among those I have been able to find) mentioned the scene beyond praising the singer performing Aksinia's role, it seems unlikely that Shostakovich or any of the opera directors with whom he worked regarded this scene as likely to cause offense.

By the time *Lady Macbeth* was staged in January 1934, the Soviet cultural landscape had undergone dramatic change, with the proletarian organizations liquidated and a union structure imposed that drew all former factions together. This meant that *Lady Macbeth* initially benefited from a cessation of press hostilities, and although, as we saw in the previous chapter, former Russian Association of Proletarian Musicians members may have resented Shostakovich's success (and the loss of their own former power), the popularity of the new opera was such that only a blow from the very top could dislodge it from its position as a pinnacle of Soviet musical achievement.

Although the *Zhenotdel* had been abolished and there were signs of change in the way the Soviet leadership regarded women's rights and general sexual behaviors—homosexuality was made illegal in 1934 and pornography in 1935, for instance—this ideological shift had not yet begun to seep into Soviet art. It is clear from the reviews of *Lady Macbeth* that critics found Shostakovich's overall message and its execution broadly successful and ideologically appropriate. As we saw in the previous chapter, Zaslavsky's hostile review of the opera's musical language and its adaptation of Leskov was not typical. Zaslavsky also made no complaint about the opera's sexual content beyond a snide comment about the prominence of the bed in the staging and "coarse naturalism" at certain points in the score, but there was no complaint about the sex itself, nor about Aksinia's assault. The truth is that had Stalin not gone to see it, the opera would have continued its successful run and, assuming that the cultural purge that the "Muddle" editorial precipitated was preordained, another target would have been found to initiate it. The freshly appointed chair of the new Committee on Arts Affairs, Platon Kerzhentsev, would have found another way to make his mark and, eventually, to bring about Meyerhold's destruction. Shostakovich might even have completed the tetralogy of operas about women that he had initially promised.[29]

Without this inflammatory back story, *Lady Macbeth* as we know it today would probably never have come about. If it survived in repertoire at all, it would most likely have done so in the form of the 1935 Muzgiz authorized score. The temptation to retrospectively identify where a Soviet composer "went wrong" must be resisted, for Shostakovich was politically astute, responded sensitively to cultural shifts, and had not the slightest desire to court controversy beyond prodding a few egos within the Composers' Union. *Lady Macbeth* fell victim not only to cultural changes with regard to artistic modernity (especially vis-à-vis "the West") and to the role of women in Soviet society but also to the formation of the Committee on Arts Affairs itself and the ambition of its new chair. It was also not helped by the clumsy attempts of Leningrad culture officials trying to boost their own friends and institutions with Stalin directly: a horrible sequence of bad luck, bad timing, and cynical opportunism.

Of all the attempts to identify and work around the ethical and dramatic flaws in *Lady Macbeth*, that of Nikolai Smolich's Maly production has the most potential for directors today, for it preserves nearly all the music intact, cutting only a few musically insignificant lines of dialogue between Katerina and Sergei. To make this work, however, audiences would not see the sex scene itself, and in today's culture of maximizing shock onstage, it is uncertain whether or not this would be accepted or derided as puritanical. In any case, it would surely be a positive step to acknowledge that the "original" *Lady Macbeth* existed in several different versions, and opera directors should be free to select from any of them.

CHAPTER 5

POSTLUDE

LADY MACBETH TODAY

IT WAS, AS I have argued, both Solomon Volkov's *Testimony* and the "origin story" of *Lady Macbeth* that have made it one of the most-performed twentieth-century operas of our time. *Testimony* was the key that unlocked *Lady Macbeth*'s potential in the West; European critics were frequently critical of *Katerina Izmailova* whenever it was performed. Yet when *Lady Macbeth* was staged in Wuppertal in 1980, there was a sudden consensus that it was vastly superior to *Katerina Izmailova*. Given that the two operas are almost identical, the role played by politics in its reception could hardly be more glaring.

The chilly reception of *Katerina Izmailova* was especially acute in West Germany. Reviewing Bohumil Herlischka's production in Basel in 1968, one critic took the opportunity

Shostakovich's Lady Macbeth of the Mtsensk District. Pauline Fairclough, Oxford University Press.
© Oxford University Press 2025. DOI: 10.1093/9780197534977.003.0005

to recall the Yugoslav Opera production in the Holland Festival in 1963: "We were stunned by the backward-looking music of the Russian composer. . . . He decided a few years ago to publish an edited version. Who knows the true original? What is left is a mixture of sentimentality, brutality and a rhythmic drive that occasionally reminds one of Orff."[1] Another performance in Vienna in May 1968 played to a half-empty State Opera House and, as the *Pirmasenser Zeitung* critic noted, it was now Western critics who did not hold back from criticizing Shostakovich's opera, while Franz Endler in *Montag* openly judged *Katerina Izmailova* to be a bad opera.[2]

Yet there were some critics who recognized that Shostakovich's revision was not a radical rewrite. Reviewing the Covent Garden production in December 1963 (director Vlado Habunek, conductor Edward Downes), the critic of *Die Welt*, though largely sympathetic (praising the "care and empathy" of the London production), found that in revising *Lady Macbeth* Shostakovich had not altered the opera significantly, presumably basing this on hearing the original, perhaps as recently as 1959 in Düsseldorf.[3] London critics concurred: several had even seen the Leningrad production in 1934 or 1935 yet mostly failed to realize that the sex scene had been cut.[4] This probably echoed the publicity materials for the production, including essays in the program booklet, which gave the misleading impression that all Shostakovich had done was to write two new entr'actes, "cleaned up" the libretto, and made some alterations to tessitura. No mention at all was made of the cut to the sex scene; in fact, the music critic Martin Cooper's introductory note to the Royal Opera House program booklet stated: "The revision concerns the verbal rather than the musical text. The crudely erotic character of some passages in the libretto has been modified and this has in one case slightly changed the character of a whole scene (Act Two Scene 1)."[5] Cooper here alludes to the removal of Katerina's impulsive demands for kisses "till the blood rushes to my head, so that the icons fall from the walls," but says nothing at all about the excision of the sex scene in Act One.

Many reviewers of European productions of *Katerina Izmailova* from the 1960s and '70s voiced criticism of Shostakovich's writing, citing his "trivial" or "operetta-like" characterization, and the difficulty in believing in Katerina as a sympathetic heroine. Although some critics mentioned the "Muddle instead of music" debacle, none did so in a manner that implied Shostakovich had been forced to revise the opera nor complained that, with the sex scene cut, it had been "castrated"—the term used by one German critic when reviewing the Wuppertal stage premiere of the revived *Lady Macbeth* in 1980.[6] Such loaded language appeared only with the prompting of *Testimony* from 1980 onward. *Katerina Izmailova*, then, although enjoying some success, was not in general held to be a masterpiece in European critical circles. Without the impact of *Testimony* and Rostropovich's recording, it may well have faded from repertoire. It is not even certain that Rostropovich's recording alone could have clinched *Lady Macbeth*'s reputation had it not been for the sensation caused by *Testimony*.

Using one London music critic to illustrate my point, let us examine a relatively rare case: someone who reviewed *Lady Macbeth*, *Katerina Izmailova*, and the all-new (Rostropovich-Sikorski) *Lady Macbeth* again within a relatively short time period (seventeen years). Peter Heyworth of the *Observer* reviewed the 1959 Düsseldorf *Lady Macbeth*, Covent Garden's 1963 *Katerina Izmailova*, and the English National Opera's 1987 *Lady Macbeth*. Heyworth had these harsh words for the Düsseldorf opera: "Alas, condemnation in *Pravda* is no surer guarantee of genius than condemnation in *The Times*, and 'Lady Macbeth' is not a masterpiece."[7] A few years later, reviewing *Katerina Izmailova* in London, he is no more complimentary, though at least he noticed that the sex scene had been cut ("he has deleted a piece of erotic music that served only to underline a situation that was already quite clear enough"); his overall criticism of both versions was that Katerina was simply not credible as a tragic victim.[8] However, his tone changed dramatically in 1987. Not only does he open the review with an account of how, owing to Stalin's reaction, the "world has lost what might have developed into the outstanding operatic talent of his generation" but also he described *Katerina Izmailova* as a "revised and milder version" and claims the score of the original version has only emerged in recent years, although what he heard at the English National Opera would probably have been exactly what he had heard in Düsseldorf.[9]

Although Heyworth holds to his first opinion that Katerina was not a believable operatic heroine, the shift in emphasis from his review in 1960 to that of 1987 is very noticeable. In 1960 he felt able to point out, as honestly and directly as he wished, exactly why he felt *Lady Macbeth* was not a masterpiece. In 1987, still maintaining that it "may not rank among the masterpieces of twentieth-century opera," his review nevertheless led with a reflection on the impact

Stalin's censure had had on the young Shostakovich in 1936 and pondered the loss of creative independence he had suffered in consequence. Heyworth had not really changed his mind, but his personal sympathies had been engaged by the post-*Testimony* critical landscape, and merely voicing an aesthetic judgment was no longer possible for him. His shift in tone is not disingenuous but rather illustrates the way in which critical narratives about *Lady Macbeth* were almost instantly intertwined with *Testimony*'s reception.

These few examples suffice to illustrate that Cold War politics played a substantial role in the success of *Lady Macbeth*. Where this leaves future productions of the opera is of course in the hands of directors, conductors, and opera house management. All parties need to consider marketing and box office—but given the highly repressive climate in Russia today, and its full-scale invasion of Ukraine in 2022, there are additional political angles to consider. A relaunch of *Katerina Izmailova* on ethical grounds would be a hard sell, to say the least, since that is the version regularly performed in Putin's Russia, where even a ballet celebrating Rudolf Nureyev has had to be canceled, such is the state-driven hostility toward LGBTQ+ citizens.[10] Although *Katerina Izmailova* is more dramatically logical and removes the dubious sexual ethics that the older Shostakovich found unacceptable, there might be little appetite now for reviving it, or for insisting on such a substantial cut to *Lady Macbeth* as to remove the postcoital dialogue, as Smolich had suggested. After all, opera aficionados are well used to accommodating bumpy corners in plots, and those snatches of awkward dialogue pass quickly.

As I have noted, the approach taken by several opera directors since 1980 has been to interpret the Act One sex scene as a mutual display of passion, often using clever lighting effects to avoid trying to stage a shift from assault to consensual sex: as can be seen from the clip of the 1980 Spoleto performance online, the stage darkens as Sergei pushes Katerina onto the bed, and the postcoital scene is sensitively staged, making the awkward dialogue easy to ignore. Martin Kušej's 2006 Dutch National Opera production also plays with lighting effects to disguise the same shift, leaving the audience with the impression of consensual sex that only begins roughly. Calixto Bieito's 2014 Flanders Opera production achieves a similar effect here through different means: guiding Katerina and Sergei's physical struggle through a process of gradual (though fast) implied consent. Richard Jones's 2004 Royal Opera House production introduced a comedic element by having the sex take place behind a shaking wardrobe, the descending trombone glissandi coinciding with the door slowly swinging open. There is no place for audience disquiet over the bizarre dialogue that follows, because attention is so strongly focused on the comedy that no disjunction is felt.

And perhaps that is the best we can hope for with this scene. Smolich's complete excision of the postcoital dialogue is a good solution and remains one possible way of making the scene more dramatically logical, removing the problematic text, and enabling directors, singers, and audiences to imagine Katerina and Sergei drawing closer. But cutting the sex scene in the manner of *Katerina Izmailova* is probably not going to be seriously considered: the charge of Stalinist (or Putinist) levels of puritanism would be too easily leveled.

As for the scene with Aksinia, there are, as we have seen, grounds for believing that Shostakovich never intended this to signify rape: had the barrel rolling been intended as a rape metaphor, Katerina's joining in the men's laughter would render her less sympathetic, despite the aspect of class distinction that may make us suspect Katerina might view the rape of a servant as fundamentally unshocking.[11] Additionally, I believe that, unpleasant though it is to admit, Shostakovich, Preis, and Smolich deliberately cast Aksinia in an unattractive light to reduce her to a "fat, gossipy peasant woman" stereotype who would be less likely to trigger a sympathetic response in the Leningrad audience. The scene was not intended to be as shocking as we now see it staged: at the very least, it should be possible for directors who wish to step back from this level of violence to do so with a firm justification, and Angelina Nikonova's production in Hamburg (2023) has done this, with Aksinia shoved into a giant pickle barrel and humiliated by various substances being poured onto her. Though Nikonova believed the original barrel rolling was intended as a metaphor for rape, her decision to stage it using a different metaphor was not because she believed the attack on Aksinia was supposed to be relatively harmless, but because of consideration for her audience.[12]

Whether opera directors, singers, and audiences continue to move away from tolerating graphic sexual violence onstage remains to be seen. Justifiably or not, *Lady Macbeth* has so far avoided such controversy, and outside Russia, this is probably at least in part because of its history of suppression under Stalin. Nevertheless, the opera is a contemporary classic, frequently performed and now almost a century old. We should not be afraid of pointing out its problems, nor of suggesting solutions. At the very least, I would argue that it is time for opera directors and conductors to step away from this reflexive acceptance of the mythologized "original" score and to stop assuming that by performing it they are realizing Shostakovich's true intentions. Notwithstanding the brilliance of many modern productions, it is perhaps also time for the ethical and dramatic flaws in this youthful masterpiece to be addressed with the same boldness that the opera's first directors, Vladimir Nemirovich-Danchenko and Nikolai Smolich, applied when considering how best to cope with these moments. I hope that by showing how the first directors recognized and managed them, future directors of *Lady Macbeth* will feel empowered to make similarly informed decisions.

ADDITIONAL SOURCES FOR READING AND LISTENING

M ANY OF THE MOST useful English-languages resources on Shostakovich are by now several decades old, but they are still essential for anyone wishing to learn more about the composer and Soviet cultural history. Laurel Fay's biography, *Shostakovich: A Life* (Oxford University Press, 2000), remains the definitive resource for anyone wanting reliable information on the facts of Shostakovich's career; my short biography *Dmitry Shostakovich* (Reaktion Books "Critical Lives," 2019) brings some information up to date and adds new perspectives and sources, but anyone seriously interested in Shostakovich will need Fay's work as the essential reference source. Similarly, Elizabeth Wilson's collection of memoirs from Shostakovich's friends and family, *Shostakovich: A Life Remembered* (Faber, 2006), offers rich, often contradictory perspectives on the composer, guided by Wilson's informed introductions to each section. A final indispensable resource on Shostakovich is the translated collection of his letters to his close friend Isaak Glikman, dating from World War II and evacuation period to the end of Shostakovich's life (*Story of a Friendship:*

The Letters of Dmitry Shostakovich to Isaak Glikman with a Commentary by Isaak Glikman, trans. Anthony Phillips, Faber, 2001). These give intimate, often moving insight into the composer's thoughts and feelings that cannot be found anywhere else.

For some up-to-date context on Soviet musical history during the Lenin and Stalin eras, I recommend Marina Frolova-Walker and Jonathan Walker's *Music and Soviet Power 1917–1932* (Boydell Press, 2012) and my own *Classics for the Masses: Shaping Soviet Musical Identity Under Lenin and Stalin* (Yale, 2016). Both give broad panoramas of the challenges of shaping a creative career under communism, while also showing the excitement and optimism of the first few decades, before Stalin's program of mass arrests brought genuine debate about the future of art and music in the new society to an end.

The best available performance of *Lady Macbeth* on CD is still Mstislav Rostropovich's landmark EMI recording of 1979, which was released on EMI Classics as a CD in 1993 and re-released in 2002 on the same label and most recently on Warner Classics in 2016. *Katerina Izmailova* has been recorded on CD but is hard to find; I direct readers therefore to the film version, with Galina Vishnevskaya in the title role, directed by Mikhail Shapiro, and available on the Lenfilm website, searchable via standard search engines, and also linked to the companion website for this book. The best available DVD recording is, in my view, that of the Dutch National Opera production of 2006, directed by Martin Kušej, with Eva-Maria Westbroek in the title role, and conducted by Mariss Jansons.

NOTES

INTRODUCTION

1. Richard Taruskin, "Entr'acte: The Lessons of *Lady M*," in *Defining Russia Musically*, ed. Taruskin (Princeton, NJ: Princeton University Press, 1997), 498–510.
2. For the best available summary of these years with specific reference to music, see Marina Frolova-Walker and Jonathan Walker, *Music and Soviet Power 1917–1932* (Woodbridge: Boydell Press, 2012).
3. Laurel Fay, *Shostakovich: A Life* (New York: Oxford University Press, 2000), 55–56.
4. Robert Conquest, *The Great Terror: Stalin's Purge of the 1930s* (Oxford: Oxford University Press, 1968).
5. Dmitri Shostakovich, *Lady Macbeth of Mtsensk*, cond. Mstislav Rostropovich, with the London Philharmonic Orchestra and Ambrosian Opera Chorus (EMI Classics, 1979).
6. Anon., "Sumbur vmesto muzyki," *Pravda*, January 28, 1936, 3.
7. Originally published by New York Harper and Row in 1979, throughout this study I will be referring to the following edition: Solomon Volkov, *Testimony: The Memoirs of Dmitri Shostakovich as related to and edited by Solomon Volkov* (London: Faber and Faber, 1981). Those interested in this book—itself a fascinating read, despite its doubtful provenance—should familiarize themselves with Laurel E. Fay, "Volkov's *Testimony* Reconsidered," in *A Shostakovich Casebook*, ed. Malcolm H. Brown (Bloomington: Indiana University Press, 2004), 22–66.
8. Volkov, *Testimony*, 86.
9. Solomon Volkov, "Tradition Returns: Rostropovich's Symbolism," in *Shostakovich Reconsidered*, ed. Allan Ho and Dmitry Feofanov (London: Toccata Press, 1998), 365. The interview with Rostropovich

was originally published in Russian in 1982 (Solomon Volkov, "O Sergee Sergeeviche i Dmitrii Dmitrieviche," *Chast' rechi* 1981/2, nos. 2–3 [1982]: 254–62). It is not quite clear what Rostropovich is referring to when he says "the revival," but he could not have been describing his own EMI version, because he immediately took action to lobby for a "third" version already in the 1960s. What his idea of a third version may have included and omitted can only be a matter for speculation.

10. A short clip of the Spoleto performance can be seen online: see online resources in the accompanying website. I am grateful to Mr. Badea for sharing his recollections of this production with me in personal conversation, November 18, 2022.

CHAPTER 1

1. A sample of post-1979 reviews makes this clear: "charged with a sensuality so strong that it could not be tolerated in the Stalin era" (Mario Pasi, "A Spoleto la 'Macbeth' che non piaceva a Stalin," *Corriera della sera*, June 27, 1980); "Stalin rejected Shostakovich because he alluded to certain realities" (Daniele Spini, "Ma Stalin rifiutó Sciostakovic perché alludeva a certe realtà," *La Nazione*, June 27, 1980); "the opera electrified its first audiences in both Russia and the West with its sexual frankness. . . . It offended the delicate sensibilities of the Soviet commissars, who denounced it in *Pravda* as 'Muddle instead of Music'" (Michael Walsh, "Add One to the List of Greats," *Time*, October 5, 1981); "Criticism was first and foremost triggered by the crude verisimilitude of the love scene between Katerina and Sergey, with its pounding, hammering 'coitus music'" (Gerhard R. Koch, "Schostakowitsches Masken und ihre Legende," *Frankfurter Allgemeine Zeitung*, February 28, 1980).

2. Fay, *Shostakovich*, 77, and Andrei Kriukov, "Put' ot 'Ledi Makbet' k 'Katerine Izmailovoi,'" in *Dmitrii Shostakovich. Issledovaniia i materialy*, ed. Ol'ga Digonskaia and Liudmila Kovnatskaia (Moscow: DSCH, 2007), 2:209–41, 220.

3. Nelli Kravets, *Riadom s velikami. Atovm'ian i ego vremia* (Moscow: GITIS, 2012), 224. The special concert was to have included the First Symphony and Piano Concerto.

4. See Elizabeth Wilson, *Shostakovich: A Life Remembered* (London: Faber, 2006), 130.

5. For this anecdote, see Isaak Glikman, *Story of a Friendship: The Letters of Dmitri Shostakovich to Isaak Glikman*, trans. Anthony Phillips (London: Faber, 1993), 215.

6. Ibid., 220.

7. Ivan Sollertinskii, speech at Leningrad Composers' Union, conference held over four days, February 21–26, 1936, reported in *Sovetskaia muzyka* 5 (1936): 41–42. For the unexpurgated stenogram of this meeting, see Nina Griaznova, "Tvorcheskaia diskussiia v Leningradskom soiuze sovetskikh kompozitorov," in *Shostakovich-Urtext*, ed. Marina Rakhmanova (Moscow: GTsMMK, 2006), 312–548.

8. For listings of operas performed at the Bolshoi from 1917, see V. V. Fedorov, *Repertuar Bol'shogo teatr SSSR, 1776–1955* (New York: Norman Ross Publishing, 2001). For further information on Wagner performances in the Soviet Union, see Rosamund Bartlett, *Wagner in Russia* (Cambridge: Cambridge University Press, 1995) and Pauline Fairclough, "Wagner Reception in Stalinist Russia," in *The Legacy of Richard Wagner*, ed. Luca Sala (Turnhout: Brepols, 2012), 309–26.

9. Fay, *Shostakovich*, 56–57.

10. See Frolova-Walker and Walker, *Music and Soviet Power 1917–1932*, 120–22.

11. For excellent contemporary discussion of all these works, see Frolova-Walker and Walker, *Music and Soviet Power*.

12. "Defamiliarization" is the term most familiar to Western readers and is taken from the techniques of Bertolt Brecht. The equivalent Soviet term was *ostraneniie*, meaning "making strange," and this was explicitly used by Meyerhold's theater.

13. For writings on Meyerhold, see Edward Braun, *Meyerhold: A Revolution in Theatre* (London: Methuen, 1998) and Braun, ed. and trans., *Meyerhold on Theatre* (London: Bloomsbury, 2016). See also Alma Hanson Law, "A Reconstruction of Meyerhold's Production *Woe to Wit*: The Relation between Literary Text and Theatrical Representation" (Ph.D. diss., Columbia University, 1977).

14. Fay, *Shostakovich*, 91–92. For his letters to Sollertinskii, see Dmitrii Sollertinskii, Liudmila Mikheeva, Galina Kopytova, Ol'ga Dansker, and Liudmila Kovnatskaia, eds., *Pis'ma I. I. Sollertinskomu* (St. Petersburg: Kompozitor, 2006).

15. Aleksandr Preis was a successful Soviet dramatist who had already worked with Shostakovich on his first opera *The Nose*.

16. Dmitrii Shostakovich, "Ledi Makbet Mtsenskogo uezda," *Sovetskoe iskusstvo*, no. 47 (1932): 3.

17. This is the translation by Joan Pemberton Smith in the 1979 EMI recording. A "bob" is a colloquial English term for money.

18. See the testimony of former Ukrainian activist Izrail Chernitskii in the PBS/BBC documentary *People's Century*, part 3, *Red Flag* (first broadcast BBC September 26, 1995), from 28:00. The interview can also be heard here: https://www.pbs.org/wgbh/peoplescentury/episodes/redflag/.

19. Shostakovich, "Moe ponimanie 'Ledi Makbet,'" *Ledi Makbet Mtsenskogo Uezda* [Programme] (Leningrad: Gosudarsvennii Akademicheskii Malyi Opernyi Teatr, 1934), 6–9; "O moey opera," *Katerina Izmailova. Libretto* (Moscow: Muzgiz, 1934), 11–13.

20. Shostakovich, "O moei opere," 11.

21. See Caryl Emerson, "Shostakovich and the Russian Literary Tradition," in *Shostakovich and His World*, ed. Laurel Fay (Princeton, NJ: Princeton University Press, 2004), 183–226, and Taruskin, "*Entr-acte:* The Lessons of Lady M."

22. Shostakovich, "Moe ponimanie 'Ledi Makbet,'" 7.

23. On February 17, 1936, the anonymous author of a piece in *Sovetskoe iskusstvo* covering the creative discussions in Moscow actually named Ostretsov directly, noting that "some of our composers . . . and musicologists (for example Ostretsov) did not reveal their own attitude in any way and refrained from taking part in the discussions." Anon., "Diskussiia v soiuze kompozitorov," *Sovetskoe iskusstvo*, February 17, 1936.

24. Aleksandr Ostretsov, "Rossiia 40-x godov," *Katerina Izmailova. Libretto* (Moscow: Muzgiz, 1934), 5–7, and "Muzyka opery," 8–10.

25. Aleksandr Ostretsov, "Ledi Makbet Mtsenskogo Uezda," *Sovetskaia muzyka* 6 (1933): 25. For a superb rebuttal of the notion that Shostakovich's approach to Katerina was Dostoevskian, see Caryl Emerson, "Back to the Future: Shostakovich's Revision of 'Lady Macbeth of Mtsensk District,'" *Cambridge Opera Journal* 1, no. 1 (1989): 59–78, especially 77.

26. See Elizabeth Wilson, *Shostakovich: A Life Remembered* (London: Faber, 2006), 114. See especially n. 127, where Shostakovich writes in frustration to Smolich that the singers playing Sonyetka made her "a female vampire" instead of a "simple, flirtatious girl, without any demoniacal side to her."

27. Valer'ian Bogdanov-Berezovskii, "Ledi Makbet Mtsenskogo Uezda," review of the premiere at Leningrad's Malyi Teatr, *Sovetskoe iskusstvo*, no. 7 (February 11, 1934): 3.

28. Ostretsov, "Katerina Izmailova v Teatre im. Nemirovicha-Danchenko," *Sovetskaia muzyka* 5 (1934): 32–33. Note that this production used the alternative title *Katerina Izmailova* to distinguish it from the co-running Leningrad staging.

29. By 1935 Gorodinskii had risen to the post of head of the Arts Section of the Central Committee of the Communist Party, a position he held until 1937. Kul'tpros = Otdel' kul'turno-prosvetitelnoi raboty (department for cultural-educational work).

30. Vladimir Iokhel'son and Viktor Gorodinskii, "Za bol'shevistkuiu samokritiku na muzykal'nom fronte," *Sovetskaia muzyka* 5 (1934): 7.

31. See Pauline Fairclough, *Classics for the Masses: Shaping Soviet Musical Identity Under Lenin and Stalin* (New Haven and London: Yale University Press, 2016), 109.

32. Iokhel'son and Gorodinskii, "Za bol'shevistskuiu samokritiku," 10.

33. Ibid.

34. Vladimir Iokhel'son, "Leningradskii sovetskikh kompozitorov k 17 s"ezdu partii," *Sovetskaia muzyka* 1 (1934): 17.

35. This abusive term was alluded to in one of the many speeches made attacking Sollertinsky in the Composers' Union discussions in February 2016. See the speech by Lev Knipper in *Sovetskaia muzyka* 3 (1936): 24.

36. Iokhel' son and Gorodinskii, "Za bol'shevistskuiu samokritiku," 8.

37. See Fairclough, *Classics for the Masses*, 101–39 for accounts of this repertoire and its reception.

38. For the best available account of this factionalism and its impact on Soviet musical life in the late 1920s and early '30s, see Frolova-Walker and Walker, *Music and Soviet Power*.

39. Sheila Fitzpatrick, *The Cultural Front: Power and Culture in Revolutionary Russia* (Ithaca and London: Cornell University Press, 1992), 203.

40. My sweep of the Soviet music press has not been fully comprehensive owing to the current impossibility of Russia-based research—but over the course of the two years of *Lady Macbeth*'s run in both cities, I did not find a single review that could be described as negative until after January 28, 1936.

41. M. (Mattias) Grinberg, "Opera i kompozitor," in "Ledi Makbet Mtsenskogo Uezda," *Sovetskoe iskusstvo*, no. 47 (1932): 3.

42. Ibid.

43. M. (Mattias) Grinberg, "Ekaterina Izmailova: opera i spektakl'," *Sovetskoe iskusstvo*, no. 44 (1932): 4.

44. Ibid.

45. Georgii Polianovskii, "Muzykal'nie prem'ery," *Rabochii i teatr*, no. 5 (February 1934): 16.

46. Ibid.

47. Evgenii Braudo, "Pobeda sovetskoi muzyki," *Literaturnaia gazeta*, no. 10 (1934): 4. Meyerhold in 1934 was still a very powerful leading figure in the arts world; his persecution and the use of "Meyerholdism" as a serious criticism dates from early 1936.

48. See the memoir of Sergei Radamsky, who sat with Shostakovich during the ill-fated Bolshoi performance attended by Stalin. He notes that the bed in Act Two was a straw mattress right at the front of the stage, while in Leningrad it was much more discreetly positioned. See Sergei Radamsky, "Lady Macbeth Put On for Stalin—But Shostakovich Waited in Vain for a Call," *The Times*, November 18, 1963, 14.

49. I am indebted to Olesia Bobrik for this information.

50. Olesia Bobrik, "Osushchestvlennïe i neosushchestvlennïe prem'erï sochineniy D. D. Shostakovicha v Bol'shom teatre: konets 1920s-mid-1930s. Kommentarii k notam iz Arkhiva Notnoy biblioteki Bol'shogo teatra Rossii," *Sovremennie problemï muzïkoznaniya*, no. 4 (2018): 127–47, at 146.

51. Kravets, *Riadom s velikimi*, 223.

52. Leonid Maksimenkov claims that Meyerhold was the intended victim from the start: see Maksimenkov, *Sumbur vmesto muzyki: Stalinskaia kul'turnaia revoliutsiia 1936–1938* (Moscow: Iuridicheskaia kniga, 1997), 19.

53. Solomon Volkov, *Testimony*, 85–86.

54. Evgenii Efimov, "Perepiska D. I. Zaslavskogo i M. M. Grinberga," *Nashe nasledie*, no. 105 (2013), accessed April 13, 2023, http://www.nasledie-rus.ru/podshivka/10513.php. See also Efimov, *Sumbur vokrug "sumbura" i odnogo "malen'kogo zhurnalista"* (Moscow: "Flinta," 2006) and Vladimir Abirinov, "Mutnyi ruchei i porochnaia ledi: kak nachinalas' travlia Shostakovicha," accessed April 13, 2023, https://www.svoboda.org/a/30402533.html. See the accompanying website for this book for live links. The instruction to Zaslavsky to include "Meyerholdism" in his critique reinforces Maksimenkov's contention that the theater director was the ultimate intended target.

55. Efimov, "Perepiska D. I. Zaslavskogo i M. M. Grinberga."

56. The second editorial attacking Shostakovich's music was "Baletnaia fal'sh" (Balletic falseness), a critical review of his third ballet, *The Limpid Stream*. *Pravda*, February 6, 1936, 3.

57. Ibid.

58. Maksimenkov, *Sumbur vmesto muzyki: Stalinskaya kul'turnaya revoliutsiya 1936–1938* (Moscow: Yuridicheskaya kniga, 1997), 14.

59. Ekaterina Vlasova, *1948 god v sovetskoi muzyke,. Dokumentirovannoe issledovanie* (Moscow: Klassika— XXI, 2010), 163.

60. Maksimenkov, *Sumbur*, 77 and 82.

61. For Stalin's approval of *Tikhii Don*, see Fay, *Shostakovich*, 84.

62. "Report from the GUGB NKVD SSSR Secret Political Department on responses from writers and arts workers to articles in Pravda about the composer D. D. Shostakovich" (no later than February 11, 1936), in Andrey Artizov and Oleg Naumov, *Soviet History and Power: A History in Documents 1917–1953*, trans. and ed. Katerina Clark and Evgeny Dobrenko (New Haven and London: Yale University Press, 2007), 234.

63. See Wilson, *Shostakovich: A Life Remembered*, 127–70; Fay, *Shostakovich*, 87–105; and Glikman, *Story of a Friendship*, 213–24.

64. Anon., "Sobranie Leningradskikh kompozitorov i muzykal'nikh kritikov," *Pravda*, February 10, 1936, 3.

65. Ivan Dzerzhinskii, "Tvorcheskaia diskussiia moskovskikh kompozitorov," *Izvestiia*, February 14, 1936, 4.

66. Genrikh Neigauz, "O prostote v iskusstve," *Sovetskoe iskusstvo*, February 17, 1936, 1.

67. Archive references as follows: RGALI f. 2048, op. 1, ed. khr. 159; Arkhiv D. D. Shostakovicha, f. 10, raz. 3, ed. khr. 433 and f. 10, raz. 3, ed. khr. 250.

68. Glikman's indispensable account reveals that only one Leningrad branch member—the composer Vladimir Shcherbachev—abstained from voting in favor.

69. Anon., "Baletnaia fal'sh'," *Pravda*, February 6, 1936, 3; Anon., "Maznia vmesto risunkov," *Komsomolskaia Pravda*, February 15, 1936; Anon., "Grubaia schema vmesto istoricheskoi pravdy," *Pravda*, February 13, 1936.

70. For a summary of these events, see Pauline Fairclough, *Dmitry Shostakovich* (London: Reaktion Books), 50–64. On Meyerhold's fate, see Vitaly Shentalinsky, *The KGB's Literary Archive* (London: Harvill Press, 1995). For an up-to-date account of Stalin's repressions, see James R. Harris, *The Anatomy of Terror: Political Violence Under Stalin* (New York: Oxford University Press, 2013), and on 1937 specifically, see Vadim Rogovin, *1937: Stalin's Year of Terror*, trans. Frederick S. Choate (Oak Park, MI: Mehring Books, 1998).

CHAPTER 2

1. I will cite just two (among many) examples of the critical conflation of Rostropovich's *Lady Macbeth* and *Testimony*: Edward Greenfield, "Crimes of Passion," *The Guardian*, May 26, 1979, 10, and Harlow Robinson, "The Politics of Lady Macbeth," San Francisco opera program booklet, San Francisco Opera, 1981, 27–34 and 71–73. Almost all substantial post-*Testimony* reviews of *Lady Macbeth* from the 1980s either show knowledge of *Testimony* or explicitly mention it.

2. Irina Levasheva, "First Edition of Dmitri Shostakovich's opera *Lady Macbeth of the Mtsensk District* (1930–1932)," in Shostakovich, *Lady Macbeth of the Mtsensk District*, New Collected Works (Moscow: DSCH Publishing, 2007), 52b;382.

3. This score is kept in the Russian State Archive of Literature and Art, f. 2048, op. 2, ed. khr. 32–35. Owing to Russia's invasion of Ukraine and resulting economic and cultural sanctions, it is not possible to gain permission from state archives to show images. All material from Russia that I collected for this research was gathered either before or during the pandemic and before February 2022. However, a single page from this score showing Shostakovich's crossing-out can be seen in the New Collected Works score of *Katerina Izmailova* (Moscow: DSCH Publishing, 2016), 59:414.

4. Anon., "Sumbur vmesto muzyki," *Pravda*, January 28, 1936, 3. I have used the translation from Victor Seroff, *Dimitri Shostakovich: The Life and Background of a Soviet Composer* (New York: Alfred A. Knopf, 1943), 204–7.

5. Ibid., 206. For the full text in English translation, see online resources in the accompanying website.

6. See Ol'ga Digonskaia, "'Ledi Makbet' i Bol'shoi teatr: na podstupakh k 'lushchemu opernomu teatru v mire," *Dmitrii Shostakovich: Issledovaniia i materialy* 4 (2012): 85–101, and especially 92, where Shostakovich's prescient fear that officials would attend and dislike his opera is described.

7. Sergei Radamsky, "Lady Macbeth Put On for Stalin—But Shostakovich Waited in Vain for a Call," *The Times*, November 18, 1963, 14.

8. Yevgeniy Yefimov, *Sumbur vokrug "sumbura" i odnogo "malen'kogo zhurnalista"* (Moscow: "Flinta"), 2006, and Vladimir Abirinov, "Mutnyi ruchei i porochnaia ledi: kak nachinalas' travlia Shostakovicha," accessed April 13, 2023, https://www.svoboda.org/a/30402533.html. See also "Perepiska D. I. Zaslavskogo i M. M. Grinberga," *Nashe nasledie*, no. 105 (2013), accessed April 13, 2023, http://www.nasledie-rus.ru/podshivka/10513.php.

9. See file "Repertuar Bol'shogo teatra s 1860-1959 gg, Bol'shoi Teatr, Moscow." See also Olesia Bobrik, "Osushchestvlennye i neosushchestvlennye prem'ery sochinenii D. D. Shostakovicha v Bol'shom teatre: konets 1920s-mid-1930s. Kommentarii k notam iz Arkhiva Notnoi biblioteki Bol'shogo teatra Rossii," *Sovremennye problemy muzykoznaniia*, no. 4 (2018): 127–47, at 128–29. I thank Olesia Bobrik for showing me the original archival sources in December 2019.

10. Performance details as follows: Nemirovich-Danchenko Theater: opening night January 24, 1934, staging by Boris Mordvinov, set by Vladimir Dmitriev, conducted by Georgi Stolyarov; Leningrad's Maly Theater: opening night January 22, 1934, staging by Nikolai Smolich, set by Vladimir Dmitriev, conducted by Samuil Samosud.

11. Boris Mordvinov carried out much of the direction for this production, but Nemirovich-Danchenko undertook the major publicity work, including a filmed statement of support for Shostakovich: see clip https://www.net-film.ru/film-35791/ from 03.43.

12. Leonid Maksimenkov, *Sumbur vmesto muzyki: Stalinskaia kul'turnaia revoliutsiia 1936–1938* (Moscow: Iuridicheskaia kniga, 1997), 46. In her program essay for the 2016 Bolshoi production of *Katerina Izmailova*, Evgeniia Gaian gives March 7 as the final date for the Leningrad Maly production, but I have not been able to verify this and it seems likely to have been a mistake. See Evgeniia Gaian, "Khozhdeniia po mukam," *Katerina Ismailova*, program essay for Bolshoi theater, 2016, 27. Isaak Glikman states that after January 28 there was only one more performance at the Maly. See Glikman, *Pis'ma k drugu: Dmitrii Shostakovich-Isaaku Glikmanu* (Moscow and St. Petersburg: Kompozitor, 1993), 315.

13. Accessed August 7, 2023, https://archive.bolshoi.ru/entity/OPERA/103 178?index = 1&sa-query = леди%20макбет%20мценского.

14. See letter of March 21, 1955, in Isaak Glikman, *Story of a Friendship: The Letters of Dmitri Shostakovich to Isaak Glikman with a Commentary by Isaak Glikman*, trans. Anthony Phillips (London: Faber, 2000), 56.

15. Ibid., 58.

16. Other changes included new entr'actes between scenes 1–2 and 7–8. See Fay, *Shostakovich*, 181–87. If there were changes that Glikman suggested that Shostakovich did not accept, the record is not currently accessible; those libretto manuscripts are not held by the Shostakovich Archive in Moscow and their whereabouts are not known.

17. For the best account of these events in English, see Glikman, *Story of a Friendship*, 58 and 260–62.

18. *Katerina Izmailova* was premiered in Leningrad's Maly Theater on April 17, 1965.

19. Fay, *Shostakovich*, 238–39.

20. Galina Vishnevskaya, *Galina. A Russian Story* (London: Sceptre, 1986), 370. Izrail' Nest'ev's review of the film concludes by saying that the beauty of Shostakovich's score ought to put a decisive end to the still-heard and "unfair" opinion that it was "sumbur vmesto muzyki." See review round-up, "Katerina Izmailova," *Iskusstvo kino*, no. 1 (1967): 21.

21. Vishnevskaya, *Galina*, 368.

22. I thank Larisa Chirkova for sending me the program for this concert.

23. See Fay, *Shostakovich*, 239. La Scala had already been turned down by Shostakovich in 1958 with the same request. See Fay, "From *Lady Macbeth* to *Katerina*," 183n76.

24. Glikman, *Story of a Friendship*, 58.

25. See for example Alfons Neukirchen, "Eine russische Lulu," *Rheinische Post*, February 8, 1980, n.p. The rumor that Rostropovich had brought the original score out of the Soviet Union seemed to be circulating at the Wuppertal premiere in 1980, since several other German critics also mention this.

26. Irina Levasheva, "Textological Comments," in Shostakovich, *Lady Macbeth of the Mtsensk District*, 52b:382.

27. Richard Osborne, "Rostropovich Conducts *Lady Macbeth of Mtsensk*," liner note to Shostakovich, *Lady Macbeth of Mtsensk*, EMI Classics, 724356777620, 2002, 14. For the original sleeve note by Solomon Volkov, see Volkov, "The Return of 'Lady Macbeth,'" EMI Classics, 077774995528, 1993, 9–11 (originally published 1979).

28. Suvi Raj Grubb, *Music Makers on Record* (London: Hamish Hamilton, 1986), 200.

29. Thanks to research by Elena Petrushanskaya, who has written about *Lady Macbeth*'s performance in the Venice Biennale festival in 1947, we know

that this was not quite accurate, but since Venice was not on the opera's original tour in 1935, it was probably overlooked. See Elena Petrushanskaya, "A Forgotten Scandal: The Background and the Origin of the First Italian Stage Production of Lady Macbeth of the Mtsensk District by Shostakovich," in *Sociocultural Crossings and Borders: Musical Microhistories*, ed. R. Stanevičiūtė and R. Povilionienė (Vilnius: Lithuanian Council for Culture, 2015), 189–212.

30. Letter dated November 5, 1979. Correspondence held by Hans Sikorski, Berlin. This letter demonstrates, I think, that Shostakovich did not give Rostropovich the orchestral score before he left the Soviet Union, and Irina Shostakovich could only have done so in the late 1970s via a courier. I thank Gabriel Teschner of Sikorski/Boosey & Hawkes for his kindness in showing me the Sikorski files on *Lady Macbeth* at their office in Berlin in 2022.

31. Personal communication, April 26, 2023. Unfortunately, Universal Edition has been unable to verify this account, nor even to confirm whether or not they still hold this score.

32. See for example Aleksandr Kolesnikov, "Mstislav Rostropovich vozrozhdaet opal'nuiu operu velikogo Shostakovicha," *Izvestiia*, December 11, 1996, and Rostropovich, "Pochemu ia ispolniaiu 'Ledi Makbet,'" *Vozrozhdenie shedevra*, program booklet for concert performance at the Bol'shoi zal of the Moscow Conservatoire, November 15–17, 1996, 1–3.

33. Rostropovich had only three weeks in which to prepare all the orchestral parts. Hiring copyists to fulfill this task cost him in the region of 20,000 dollars. See letter dated November 5, 1979, to Jürgen Köchel, Archive of Hans Sikorski, Berlin.

34. Stalin's death and subsequent cultural agreements between the Soviet Union and Western nations led to major reevaluation of Shostakovich's music. For an account of how this played out in Britain, with particular attention paid to the *Testimony* effect, see Pauline Fairclough, "The 'Old' Shostakovich: Reception in the British Press," *Music & Letters* 88, no. 2 (2007): 266–96. For a recent fine study of Shostakovich's French reception, see Madeline Roycroft, "The Reception of Dmitri Shostakovich in France, 1934–2000" (Ph.D. diss., Melbourne Conservatorium of Music, 2022).

35. See especially the documentary *Shostakovich: Music in the Shadow of Stalin* by John Amis, who interviewed Maxim Shostakovich, Solomon Volkov, Edward Downes, and Mstislav Rostropovich and asked Maxim Shostakovich several questions about *Testimony*'s accuracy. Originally broadcast on BBC Radio 3 in 1968, it is now available at https://www.youtube.com/watch?v=R30XfGTI YNA. I thank Isla Baring for this information.

36. Volkov, "The Return of *Lady Macbeth*," 10–11.

CHAPTER 3

1. Laurel E. Fay, "From *Lady Macbeth* to *Katerina*. Shostakovich's Versions and Revisions," in *Shostakovich Studies*, ed. David Fanning (Cambridge: Cambridge University Press, 1994), 160–88, and Manashir Yakubov, "Explanatory Notes," in Shostakovich, *Lady Macbeth of the Mtsensk District*, New Collected Works (Moscow: DSCH Publishers, 2011), 53:621–36.

2. Galina Vishnevskaya sang the "little nest" text (with the "eternity" variant) in the film version of *Katerina Izmaylova*.

3. Shostakovich, *Lady Macbeth of the Mtsensk District*, New Collected Works, vol. 53, from 517.

4. Mikhailovskii Theatre archive, copy of *Ledi Makbet Mtsenskogo Uezda* 'edinaia-graficheskaia-dokumental'naia rezhisserskaia partitura'. I thank Ekaterina Riabkina for sending me this resource in 2021.

5. RMMK, f. 32, ed. khr. 271 contains the "colt/filly" text only; RMMK f. 32, ed. khr. 284 contains the "colt/filly" text as well, but the "little nest" text is written in pencil above the stave. Fay discusses both these scores in her chapter and reproduces Katerina's aria text in both Russian and English. In her analysis of these sources, Irina Levasheva surmises that this score was probably Melik-Pashaev's conducting score for the Bolshoi production. She also states that an additional copy of this score, held at the Shostakovich Archive, was a further copy of this one, used (according to Irina Shostakovich) by Shostakovich when he attended rehearsals at the Bolshoi and so presumably dates from late 1935. From my own examination of these sources, I can confirm that the score held in the Shostakovich Archive is indeed a further copy of RMMK, f. 32 ed., khr. 284, and that this was the version of the score used by Rostropovich in 1978 and currently held in the Sikorski Archive. In all these sources, the copyist appears to be the same person (unidentified). Irina Levasheva, "Textological Comments," in Shostakovich, *Lady Macbeth of Mtsensk*, New Collected Works, 52b:387.

6. Sergei Radamsky, "About 'Lady Macbeth'" [Letter], *New York Times*, February 17, 1935, 8.

7. Mikhailovskii Theatre archive, *Ledi Makbet Mtsenskogo Uezda*.

8. In the last recorded interview with Shostakovich in 1975, the composer claimed that these bars irritated him and distracted from the point of the scene. See editorial introduction, *Katerina Izmailova*, Sobranie Sochinenii (Moscow: Muzyka, 1985), 20:n44.

9. I am deeply grateful to Olesia Bobrik for showing me these parts when I visited the archive in December 2019.

10. I again direct readers to Fay's chapter on the different sources for this scene and her meticulous assembly of materials that show how difficult Shostakovich evidently found it to settle on a final version of this dialogue.

11. RMMK f. 32, ed. khr. 284.

12. Yakubov provides the original Preis text: "Married? I've never seen a married woman soil the bed with blood! Have you really been a virgin all this time? So if not for me . . ." (*Muzha? Shto-to ne videl ia, shtob muzhnie zheny krov'iu postel' marali! Neuzheli do sikh por devitsei byla?*), but the facsimile shows minor variation on this, and Sergei does not sing "marali" but another word that is illegible; he goes on to gloat at Zinovy rather than express amazement at Katerina's virginity. See Shostakovich, *Lady Macbeth of Mtsensk*, New Collected Works, 53:526–27.

13. Autograph B, also shown in Shostakovich, *Lady Macbeth of Mtsensk*, New Collected Works, vol. 53, restores the text "I have no husband/only you alone," cuts "Milyi!," and ends only with Sergey's "A nu, Katia!" (603).

14. A stage play adaptation of *Lady Macbeth* was actually running concurrently with the Bolshoi production in Moscow in December 1935, at the Studiia Dikogo (dir. Aleksey Dikii).

15. Manashir Yakubov, "On How *Lady Macbeth of the Mtsensk District* Was Created: Writing the Libretto," in *Ledi Makbet Mtsenskogo Uezda*, New Collected Works, 53:454. Olga Digonskaia confirms that other than the nearly complete draft, the annotated libretto documents that Yakubov used are no longer to be found in the Shostakovich Archive.

16. The production cast and crew also used copies of the Nemirovich-Danchenko score. Since there was no published orchestral score in the 1930s, conductors would all have used copyist scores, and as we have seen, at least three of these (RMMK f. 32, ed. khr. 271 and 284, plus the copyist score that Rostropovich used) gave this scene unexpurgated. I thank Olesia Bobrik and Ol'ga Digonskaia for showing me these resources.

17. As far as I am aware, the materials from Nemirovich-Danchenko's production have not been preserved. The orchestral score held in the Mariinsky Theatre library has the following archival reference: Central Music Library (Tsentral'naia muzykal'naia biblioteka) VII I III [= Shostakovich] 798, inv. 25126. The score is marked and dated as checked by Shostakovich in June–July 1933, and the copyist's name is given as "Smelik." I am indebted to Galina Kopytova for this information. Until it becomes possible for researchers both inside and outside Russia to gain access to this resource, we will never conclusively know what performance decisions Shostakovich and Samosud came to.

18. See Dan Healey, *Bolshevik Sexual Forensics: Diagnosing Disorder in the Clinic and Courtroom, 1917–1939* (DeKalb: Northern Illinois University Press, 2009), 86.

19. Nikolai Leskov, *Lady Macbeth of Mtsensk*, trans. Robert Chandler (London: Hesperus Press, 2003), 11–12.

20. Ibid., 12.

21. Yakubov, "On How *Lady Macbeth of the Mtsensk District* Was Created," 451.
22. Mikhailovskii Theatre, *Ledi Makbet*, 40.
23. Productions by David Pountney (English National Opera, 1987), Martin Kušej (Dutch National Opera, 2006), and Calixto Bieto (Flanders Opera, 2014; Geneva, 2023) all show this.

CHAPTER 4

1. Shostakovich, "Tragediia-satir," *Sovetskoe iskusstvo*, no. 47 (1932): 3.
2. The best available summary of this sudden shift can be found in Frolova-Walker and Walker, *Music and Soviet Power*, 314–23.
3. Pavla Vesela, "The Hardening of Cement: Russian Women and Modernization," *NWSA Journal* 15, no. 3 (2003): 109, quoting from Lenin's article in *Pravda*, March 4, 1920, for International Women's Day.
4. Ibid., 109.
5. Thomas D. Schrand, "Soviet 'Civic-Minded Women' in the 1930s: Gender, Class, and Industrialization in a Socialist Society," *Journal of Women's History* 11, no. 3 (1999): 126–50, 129.
6. Ibid., 130.
7. Barbara Evans Clements, "The Birth of the New Soviet Woman," in *Bolshevik Culture: Experiment and Order in the Russian Revolution*, ed. Abbott Gleason, Peter Kenez, and Richard Stites (Bloomington: Indiana University Press, 1989), 231, 233.
8. Healey, *Bolshevik Sexual Forensics*, 93.
9. Eric Naiman, *Sex in Public: The Incarnation of Early Soviet Ideology* (Princeton, NJ: Princeton University Press, 1997), 260–61. Vladimir Orlov has previously linked Naiman's account with *Lady Macbeth*: see Orlov, "Shostakovich and Soviet Eros: Forbidden Fruit in the Realm of Communal Communism," in *Contemplating Shostakovich: Life, Music and Film*, ed. Alexander Ivashkin and Andrew Kirkman (Farnham: Ashgate, 2012), 191–206.
10. Healey, *Bolshevik Sexual Forensics*, 58, and Naiman, *Sex in Public*, 283.
11. Quoted in Naiman, *Sex in Public*, 100.
12. Jennifer Louise Wilson, "Griboedov in Bed: Meyerhold's Woe to Wit and the Staging of Sexual Mores in the NEP Era," *Pushkin Review* 15 (2012): 143–60.
13. Alma Hanson Law, "A Reconstruction of Meyerhold's Production *Woe to Wit*: The Relationship between Literary Text and Theatrical Representation" (Ph.D. diss., Columbia University, 1977), 164.
14. Ibid., 94.
15. Ibid., 158.
16. Ibid., 166.

17. Pavla Vesela's study of this novel draws on all the revised editions made of this novel, right up to 1958; but for the present discussion, I will cite examples only from the late 1920s and 1939 versions. Vesela, "The Hardening of Cement," 104–23.

18. Naiman, *Sex in Public*, 95.

19. The scene is quoted at length in ibid., 177–78.

20. For example, Calixto Bieto (Geneva, 2023), Martin Kušej (Dutch National Opera, 2006), and Richard Jones (Royal Opera House, 2004).

21. In Russian, "Ish ty kuda polez," which can also mean "where are you touching me?" but expressed more strongly and colloquially, e.g., "where the hell . . . ?"

22. "Parshivyi chort, ne lez', poshel."

23. Rena Moisenko, *Realist Music* (London: Meridian Books, 1949), 204.

24. Boris Asaf'yev, "O tvorchestve Shostakovicha i ego opere 'Ledi Makbet,'" *Ledi Makbet Mtsenskogo uezda* (Leningrad: Gos. Ak. Malyi Teatr, 1934), 27–31, 30. The Russian text is: "есть баба, которую презирают за ее же физиологические свойства, и над которой насильничают." The exact word he used for rape is *nasil'nichat'*; Dan Healey confirms that the normal term used in Soviet legal texts and press reports was *iznasil'ovat'* but Asafyev's term is not ambiguous: it means rape. I thank Dan Healey for his helpful comments and suggestions; personal communication, May 24, 2023.

25. This was my impression of the revival of Calixto Bieito's 2014 Flanders production at the Grand Théâtre de Genève in April–May 2023. Bieito confirmed that during this scene he did not give the singers specific instructions, instead working together with the singers in shaping the action onstage. Personal communication, May 24, 2023.

26. The mezzo soprano Carole Wilson, who sang the role of Aksinia in this production, believes the original barrel rolling to be a metaphor for rape and is clear that Aksinia is supposed to be raped by Sergei in this scene. Personal conversation, August 8, 2023.

27. Leskov (trans. Chandler), *Lady Macbeth*, 6–7.

28. Aksinia, as the senior female member of the Izmailov household staff, held a privileged position. Even if not at the rank of the wet nurse, a figure much beloved in nineteenth-century Russian literature and culture (Tchaikovsky's opera *Eugene Onegin* providing the *locus classicus* of such a character in opera), Aksinia is shown gossiping with Katerina—an obvious indicator of rank in the household. An assault on her is appreciably different from one on a servant further down the social scale, and we can reasonably expect Katerina to have been sympathetic to her plight.

29. For this, and for the plot draft of what was intended to have been the second opera, see Fairclough, *Shostakovich*, 37–47.

CHAPTER 5

1. Anon., from Stadttheater Basel, December 27, 1968, reporting on Bohumil Herlischka's performance of *Katerina Izmailova*, "Die zweite Fassung der 'Lady Macbeth auf dem Lande,'" source unclear; archived with press cuttings in Sikorski archive, Berlin.

2. Anon., "Schostakowitsch half Wiener Oper nicht," *Pirmasenser Zeitung*, May 15, 1968, n.p.; Franz Endler, *Montag*, "Weibsteufel auf Russland," *Montag*, May 13, 1968, n.p.

3. Heinz Joachim, "Trauer und die leidende Kreatur," *Die Welt*, December 6, 1963, n.p.

4. See "A Wreath for Shostakovich" in *Tribune*, December 13, 1936 (press cutting from Royal Opera House archives, no author or page available); Dennis Gray Stoll, "Shostakovich's Katerina Izmailova," *Theatre World*, January 1964, n.p.

5. Martin Cooper, introductory note to program booklet for the Royal Opera House production, December 1963.

6. Alfons Neukirchen, "Eine russische Lulu," *Rheinische Post*, February 6, 1980, n.p.

7. Peter Heyworth, "Shostakovich's Banned Opera," *The Observer*, March 6, 1960, 23.

8. Heyworth, "Misalliance in Mtsensk," *The Observer*, December 8, 1963, 29.

9. As far as I am aware, the orchestral score sent abroad for all performances of *Lady Macbeth* in the 1930s was the unexpurgated version found by Rostropovich in the 1970s, complete with sex scene and suggestive trombone slides. References to these are to be found in US press reviews of Artur Rodziński's 1935 Cleveland performance (and later tour venues). The orchestral scores still held in Russian archives and libraries all appear to be by the same copyist who created the score used later by Rostropovich, and no copy containing any cuts has yet been found. Thus, any performance outside Russia in the 1930s, 1940s (Venice Biennale), or 1950s (Düsseldorf) would also have used this version, since no new performing parts were created from the Muzgiz 1935 score, which kept a number of cuts from the Nemirovich-Danchenko version.

10. See Ol'ga Mamikonian, "Balet 'Nureev' Serebrennikova sniali s repertuara Bol'shogo teatra iz-za zakona o LGBT," *Forbes*, April 19, 2023, https://www.forbes.ru/forbeslife/487981-balet-nureev-serebrennikova-snali-s-repertuara-bol-sogo-teatra-iz-za-zakona-o-lgbt. *Lady Macbeth* has been performed at the Bol'shoi only once since 1935 (in 2004); in 1980 and 2016, *Katerina Izmailovu* was performed there, https://archive.bolshoi.ru/entity/OPERA/.

11. Nineteenth-century Russian literature and, indeed, opera—*Eugene Onegin* being just one example—often depict the senior female servant in a

landowning household as a respected, beloved figure. Although this role is usually occupied by the wet nurse (as in *Onegin*), the Izmailov household, being childless, grants this status to Aksinia. We should not assume, therefore, that Aksinia's lower class status would make her distress invisible to Katerina, especially since her privileged position in the household has been shown by them gossiping together.

12. Personal communication, June 23, 2023.

INDEX

www.ingramcontent.com/pod-product-compliance
Ingram Content Group UK Ltd.
Pitfield, Milton Keynes, MK11 3LW, UK
UKHW022308130526
471070UK00013B/85